MAURIE

A True Story

A National General Pictures Release

Written by Douglas Morrow
Produced by Frank Ross and Douglas Morrow
Directed by Daniel Mann

STARRING

BERNIE CASEY · · · · · · · · · · · · · · · ·Maurice Stokes
BO SVENSON · · · · · · · · · · · Jack Twyman
JANET MacLACHLAN · · · · · · · · · ·Dorothy Parsons
STEPHANIE EDWARDS · · · · · · · · · · · ·Carole Twyman

Frank

MAURIE is a true story of human magnifi-cence—

The magnificence of Maurice Stokes

A routine fall on a basketball court—a week later, unable to move, to speak, to chew. Victim of a trau-matic encephalopathy, Maurie was faced with medi-cal doubt that he would ever swallow except through a siphon, much less speak, or write, or stand, even if he lived at all. But live he did, with a richness that endowed all who knew him. And, after a decade of intensely painful therapy that would have killed lesser men, *stand* he did—to receive the tumultuous ovation of the crowd attending Jack Twyman Night at the Cincinnati Gardens in March 1966.

The magnificence of Jack Twyman

A teammate of Maurie's and fellow star of the Royals—Jack saw what Maurie needed, and provided it. Legally adopting Maurie, so that he could conduct his financial affairs, was just the beginning. Maurie's therapy cost $100,000 a year. Jack Twyman raised it. For a decade. And, while continuing his demanding career as a star of the NBA gave a love and devotion to Maurie that grew in richness with the years.

The magnificence of these two extraordinary men . . . The magnificence of knowing them!

MAURIE

A TRUE STORY · BY DOUGLAS MORROW

tempo books

GROSSET & DUNLAP
A National General Company
Publishers   New York

ISBN: 0-448-05700-X

A Tempo Books Original
Tempo Books is registered in the U.S. Patent Office
Published simultaneously in Canada
Printed in the United States of America

With profound respect and deep appreciation to Maurie . . .

and to all those who knew and loved him.

MAURIE

MEDIUM SHOT—INT. DETROIT ARENA—
ON THE FLOOR—NIGHT

JACK TWYMAN has the ball. He dribbles back
and forth, laterally—his hands deftly and rhythmically controlling the ball as his massive body
moves sideways and backwards, looking for an
opening to the basket or an open man to pass the
ball to. Around him, nine men also maneuver,
some trying to set up an offensive move, others
defending against. The agility and lightning re-
flexes of these big men is stunning. It is more than
just an eye-popping demonstration of physical
prowess by trained athletes. There is, in the pat-
terns of their moves and the incredible grace and
control of their bodies, the flow and texture of a
tumultuous but disciplined ballet. The overall
visual effect is orchestrated by the alternately
descending and ascending waves of sound pro-
jected by over 10,000 engrossed spectators. Jack
stops near the top of the key, holds the ball and
pivots back and forth—

CLOSE SHOT—JACK

This is an imposing figure of a man,—220 pounds
of sinew distributed over a 6:6 frame. His eyes
flash back and forth as, panting, he studies the
alignments. It is not a conventionally handsome
face, but it reflects a strength and ruggedness that
matches his body,—a body which, loose and lithe,
reacts instantly and gracefully to whatever is re-
quired of it. The word "ROYALS" on his shirt

identifies his team. He is guarded by a "PIS-TONS". Jack feints back and forth deciding whether to step back for a jump shot,—or wheel to the side and drive in for a layup,—or pass off—

LARGER ANGLE—THE PLAY

Jack passes off to MAURIE STOKES, who is angling out from the corner. He begins to yo-yo back and forth just beyond the key, as the offensive and defensive alignments shift—

CLOSE SHOT—MAURIE

If Jack is imposing, Maurie is awesome. Six foot seven, 245 pounds,—and all of it dynamically and perfectly proportioned. This is a handsomely structured face,—dominated by large, alert and expressive eyes. As his sweat-surfaced body glistens darkly in the bright lights, Maurie reflects power and intelligence—

LARGER ANGLE—THE PLAY

As Maurie feints back and forth, Jack accelerates suddenly and wheels past him. Maurie flips the ball to Jack who stops suddenly, sets a screen which blocks off the man guarding Maurie, at the same instant passing the ball back to Maurie, who dribbles twice and drives in, unimpeded, for an easy lay-up. The ball caroms off the backboard and into the hands of a PISTONS rebounder, who starts up-court—

FULL SHOT—THE PLAYING AREA

Detroit maneuvers briefly, gets the ball to the open man who pops one in from 12 feet. The Royals bring the ball down-court. At mid-court it goes to Maurie. As he brings it up—

MEDIUM SHOT—TOWARD DETROIT BASKET

Maurie, Jack and a third Royals player go into a weave, the ball criss-crossing back and forth. As it comes to Maurie, Detroit double-teams him. Jack slips free into the corner. Maurie has a clear shot at him. He passes,—wildly. Although Jack lunges desperately, the errant pass goes past him out of bounds.

ANGLE ON ROYALS BENCH—COACH & TRAINER

The final buzzer sounds. As the players come toward the bench from the floor—

CoACH

Bus in a half-hour, snack at the airport, flight to Cincinnati at 11:30 . . .

INT. AIRLINER—NIGHT

Some of the players are sleeping, some reading, talking. Eddie, in a window seat, is asleep. Jack is beside him in the aisle seat, reading a magazine. Across the aisle, Richie is asleep in the window seat. Maurie is beside him in the aisle seat, his head against the backrest. He is awake, preoccupied with his thoughts. Jack flips the last page of the magazine, starts to put it in the slot on the back of the seat in front of him and glances toward Maurie, gesturing with the magazine. Maurie shakes his head. Jack stows the magazine, tilts his seat back and closes his eyes.

VERY CLOSE SHOT—MAURIE'S FACE

The handsome face is in repose. But there is something about those expressive eyes. Troubled? Wondering?

VERY SLOWLY, THE CAMERA MOVES TOWARD THE EYES, as if trying to capture the elusive message they seem to project. Finally, THE EYES ALONE FILL THE SCREEN.

They close.

And another pair of closed eyes DISSOLVE IN OVER THEM.

AS CAMERA HOLDS ON EYES

An alarm clock rings off-stage. The eyes pop open.

CLOSE SHOT—MAURIE (age 10)—BEDROOM—STOKES HOME—DAY

They were his eyes,—as he lies in bed with brother Harry, about 8. From the way they are snuggled under thick covers we can tell that it is cold.

MEDIUM SHOT—MAURIE & HARRY

Maurie snakes an arm out from under the covers, reaches for something on the floor—OFF CAMERA—and pulls back INTO CAMERA. He holds a battered basketball. Harry's eyes open sleepily,—and he watches as, with only his arm out from under the covers, Maurie softly flips the basketball toward the opposite wall—

FULL SHOT—THEIR ROOM

It is a small, simply furnished room,—bed, chair, bureau and table. The table is against the wall opposite the bed. On it is the ringing alarm clock. The ball lofts across the room in a wide, soft arc, hits the wall gently and drops down on to the top of the alarm clock, turning it off and knocking it over on the table.

> HARRY *(mumbling drowsily)*
> Big deal . . .

> MAURIE *(impressed with himself)*
> That was a bank shot . . .

> HARRY
> I'll clap later . . .

He goes back to sleep. As does Maurie. An instant later, Mrs. Stokes enters the room, determinedly. She has done this before. Automatically, she picks up the basketball and places it on the table. She rights the overturned clock—

MRS. STOKES

Maurie . . . I do wish you'd stop beating up on
that poor clock . . . they don't grow on trees . . .

She grabs the covers and pulls everything entirely
off the bed, as the boys shiver and squirm, wide
awake in the chill morning air.

INT. STOKES KITCHEN—DAY

The Stokes home is a small, very inexpensive house
in a poor section of Pittsburgh. It is the fruit of a
lifetime of work by Tero and Myrtle Stokes. And,
struggled for, this simple dwelling is a source of
pride and the subject of loving care. Inexpensively
but adequately furnished, it is meticulously main-
tained and reflects the character of Mr. and Mrs.
Stokes. They have confronted the diverse chal-
lenges and obstacles of their lives with conscien-
tious dignity and, through a meld of hard work
and devotion, have created for themselves and
children a very modest but very real home. Mr.
Stokes' job in the steel mill provides just enough
for the bare essentials. The only extras in this
household are love and self-respect.

Mr. Stokes, Maurie, his sister Clarice and Harry
are at breakfast,—Mrs. Stokes busy at the stove.
Maurie is attacking breakfast as if the place were on
fire. He is almost finished, as the others proceed
at a more normal pace—

MRS. STOKES

For goodness' sake, Maurie . . . chew your food.

The Lord gave you teeth . . . use them . . .

MAURIE
I'm savin' 'em for corn on the cob . . .

Clarice and Harry giggle—

MR. STOKES
Never saw you so anxious to get to school . . .

MAURIE
Joey 'n me gonna practice jump shots 'fore it opens . . .

He rises quickly from the table and grabs his books and the basketball from the kitchen counter. As he hurriedly starts off—

MR. STOKES *(quietly but firmly)*
Maurie . . .

Maurie stops. It is clear that when, on selected occasions, Mr. Stokes uses this tone the Stokes children stop and listen. Maurie waits,—impatient but respectful—

MR. STOKES
Don't mind you playin' . . . kids oughta. But studyin' comes first.

MAURIE
I done my homework . . .

CLARICE & HARRY *(in unison)*
I *did* my homework . . .

MAURIE

Okay . . . so we *all* done our homework . . .

MR. STOKES

Why is studyin' so important?

It is apparent that this is not the first time Mr.
Stokes has put Maurie through this catechism.

MAURIE

'Cause you can't make it if you're dumb.

MR. STOKES   *(shakes head)*

I learned you better'n that.

MAURIE

You always sayin' you gotta get an education to get
anywhere . . .

MR. STOKES   *(nods)*

But bein' smart or dumb's got nuthin' to do with
education. Lotta educated fellas are dumb.

HARRY

Poppa . . . you dumb or smart?

MR. STOKES   *(small thoughtful frown)*

Don't rightly know, Harry. Think maybe I might
be smart. But without education I was never able
to find out. So I had to work hard . . . hard as hell.
Lord, the years in that steel mill! I don't want any
of you to have to work like *that* . . .

CLARICE   *(shyly proud)*

We're better off than a lot of people I know . . .

MR. STOKES

Reckon so. Your mother and me survived pretty
good with a lotta hard work and not much learnin'.
Which oughta prove how much better it could be
with hard work *and* education.

MAURIE   *(pointedly wry)*

Either way, you keep talkin' about *hard work* . . .

MR. STOKES   *(grins)*

You're learnin' . . .

Maurie grins back, tucks his books under one arm
and with the other hand starts to dribble the basketball. Some fancy footwork as he yo-yos around the
kitchen table and, finally, out of the room, dribbling as he goes.

CLOSE   ANGLE—PODIUM—ST.   FRANCIS
COLLEGE—GRADUATION DAY

Father Vincent hands Maurie his diploma but, in-
stead of the usual handshake, he places his hand on
Maurie's shoulder and detains him. As the applause
dies down—

FATHER VINCENT

. . . I'm sure that no member of this graduating
class will mind if I say a special word about
Maurice, who has done so much for St. Francis. I
can only hope that we have done as much for him.
I would never have dreamed that one of our young
men would become an All-American. St. Francis is
a small, little-known college . . . or was, until

Maurice. But now, we bask in his hard-won and
much deserved glory . . .

(he smiles)

. . . I don't know much about such things, but I
am told that we should be very proud that our Big
Mo was the first draft choice of the Royals of the
National Basketball Association. And we *are* proud.
But we are even prouded of Maurice as we know
him . . . the student . . . the young man . . .

He offers his hand to Maurie, who takes it as the
applause wells up again. Maurie smiles, under-
standably pleased but a little embarrassed, and
moves off.

MEDIUM SHOT—A SEMI-SUBURBAN
STREET—NIGHT

A small car moves slowly down the street. It is a
district of contiguous, modest single-unit brick
dwellings on the edge of the urban sprawl. Each
unit boasts a small porch and a sad few feet of
lawn—

INT. CAR

BILLY is driving. Maurie is beside him on the
front seat and JIMMY beside Maurie. Three other
fellows are squeezed into the back seat. It is a very
tight fit. Except for Maurie and Billy, the four
others are slumped down, dozing—

MAURIE (dubiously)
. . . I still think you've got a helluva nerve . . .

BILLY *(confidently)*

Nah . . . she *invited* me . . .

MAURIE

You . . . not *us* . . .

BILLY

But it's a party for her cousin. You can always use some extra guys at a party . . .

Maurie glances around at the four sleeping beauties and grimaces—

MAURIE

If the party depends on these guys, the party's *dead* . . .

(glances off)

. . . 412 . . . that it?

Billy nods and looks around for a place to park—

FULL SHOT—THE STREET

Billy drives slowly, looking for an open space along the curb. He finds a small space and slowly angles back into it—

CLOSE ANGLE—THE CAR

Billy straightens his wheels and carefully inches forward. Then he backs slowly and is expertly parked,—his rear bumper having just barely touched the front bumper of a broken-down heap parked behind him. Four guys are lolling on the front stoop of a home fronting the parking space Billy has taken. When his bumper taps that of the

jalopy behind, the guys rise and move toward
Billy's car. These are rough looking mugs, obviously spoiling for some action. They all run about
6 feet and average about 200 pounds. In normal
circumstances they would be a fearsome group. As
they reach the curb—

1st GUY   *(tough)*
Okay, boy . . . outa the car! . . .

JIMMY   *(sticks head out)*
What's the problem?

1st GUY
Ya banged into my car! . . .

BILLY
I'm sure there's no damage . . .

1st GUY   *(ominous)*
Outa the car, shine . . . and there's gonna be
plenty of damage! . . .

A second guy yanks open the car door and gestures
Billy out—

2nd GUY   *(eagerly)*
Come and get your lumps, boy! . . .

Billy slowly gets out. He is about 6:3, about 215.
The four mugs are not impressed. They move
menacingly toward Billy,—as Jimmy eases out of
the car—

JIMMY   *(softly)*
Can I have some lumps, too? . . .

He stands about 6:4, maybe 225. The menacing advance slows. As it does, the three fellows in the back seat unravel themselves out of the car,—somewhat like the clowns emerging from the tiny car in the circus. They run, roughly, 6:5, 230,—6:6, 240,—6:7, 245. As they exit, they languidly form a sort of circle around the four mugs,—who suddenly seem to have shrunk and frozen. Maurie finally gets out of the car, dominating the tableau. The four mugs stare—

MAURIE *(quietly)*
You were saying something about damage?—

Staring, the first guy tries to moisten dry lips with a dry tongue. His voice has suddenly developed a crack—

1ST GUY *(finally)*
Uh . . . yeah . . . what I was sayin' was . . . uh . . . no damage at all, sir . . .

(to Billy)
. . . you park a car real good, sir . . .

BILLY *(mock-polite)*
Thanks, boy . . .

Maurie takes a languid step forward. The four mugs retreat backward toward their heap—

1ST GUY *(hastily)*
We'll move our car so you'll have more room when you leave . . . but no rush . . . stay as long as you like . . .

The four mugs hustle into the heap and take off.

> MAURIE   *(drily, to Billy)*
Nice block your girl friend lives on . . .

Billy shrugs,—glances toward the departing heap and grins—

> BILLY
They move in and the neighborhood goes to hell . . .

Laughing, the six fellows move down the street.

INT. LIVING ROOM—BILLY'S GIRL'S HOME —NIGHT

The small room is jammed,—with frenetically dancing couples and blasting stereo. Maurie stands near the doorway to the front porch, watching. Although there are perhaps a dozen couples cavorting around, Maurie's five friends dominate the scene. In the small room, these five guys look like a stand of agitated redwood trees. And they manage, somehow, in the close quarters, to make rhythmic moves that would defeat Nureyev. Billy and his partner dance close to Maurie, shaking up a storm. Maurie moves closer to the door to give them room. As he watches, grinning, he idly glances out to the porch. Something catches his attention and he moves out on to the porch—

ANGLE ON PORCH

A GIRL is on the porch, her back to the door. She

is partly bent over, head lowered, her hands on the porch railing, supporting her. She appears to be in some sort of distress. Maurie takes a couple of steps toward her—

MAURIE

You okay?

The girl nods slightly, without raising her head. Maurie moves to her—

MAURIE

You sure?

DOROTHY *(wearily)*

I'm sure . . .

She slowly straightens up and turns to face Maurie. As she does, her eyes are level with his chest. Slowly, she raises her head to stare at him—

DOROTHY *(in awe)*

Oh, God! . . . *Another* one! . . .

She swivels her head back and forth as she massages her neck with one hand.

DOROTHY

. . . And you're the biggest one of the bunch! . . .

Maurie grins and studies her. She is worth studying. An uncommonly lovely girl. Bright, warm eyes. A glowing smile. A lithe, enticing figure. Packaging that does appropriate justice to the beautiful woman within. Even in her momentary distress, as she kneads her aching neck muscles, she is radiant.

MAURIE   *(grinning)*
What's the problem?

DOROTHY
It's like dancing with a sequoia tree . . .

MAURIE
Then I won't ask you to dance.

DOROTHY
No offense . . . but thanks.

She smiles. Maurice places his hands on her lower neck. She studies him cautiously.

MAURIE
May I?

DOROTHY   *(drily)*
I don't know. What did you have in mind?

Smiling, Maurie gently massages her neck and upper shoulder. She looks up at him, a little surprised and quizzical—

DOROTHY
You're very gentle . . .

MAURIE   *(shrugging)*
Why not?

DOROTHY
Do you have any idea what it's like dancing with Billy?

MAURIE   *(grinning)*
Nope. Never danced with him.

DOROTHY   *(smiles)*
I'm Dorothy Parsons . . .

MAURIE
I'm Maurie Stokes. Sorry you're having such a lousy time.

DOROTHY
Oh, not really. But you fellows take some getting used to . . .

He stops massaging her neck, places his hands on her waist and easily lifts her to a sitting position on the porch railing. Her head is now more comfortably near level with his,—especially as he slouches down to lean on the railing.

MAURIE
That better? . . .

(she nods gratefully)
. . . You live around here?

DOROTHY   *(shaking head)*
New York. I suppose you're a basketball player, too?

MAURIE
How'd you ever figure *that* out?

DOROTHY
Should I know you?

MAURIE
Guess not.

DOROTHY

Aren't you good?

MAURIE

Know better about that in a couple of months. I report to the Royals next week. What do *you* do?

DOROTHY

Personnel work.

MAURIE   *(a little surprised)*

Where?

DOROTHY

McGraw-Hill Publishing Company.

MAURIE   *(impressed)*

Guess you'll take some getting used to, too . . .

DOROTHY

Why?

MAURIE

I'm not used to girls with muscles.

DOROTHY   *(mock resentment)*

I do *not* have muscles. A few curves perhaps . . . but no muscles.

MAURIE

You *must* have muscles . . . in your head.

Dorothy can't help being intrigued. This giant is surprisingly gentle and off-beat. For a moment, they study each other—

MAURIE

The schedule has us playing the Knicks in New York next month.

DOROTHY

I'm glad to hear that.

MAURIE

Didn't realize you were a basketball fan.

DOROTHY *(simply)*

I'm not.

MAURIE

I'll call you.

DOROTHY

I certainly hope so . . .

She smiles warmly and goes into the house.

AN ACTION MONTAGE

This will be a series of short staccato sequences showing the Royals in action against various teams of the NBA. From a particularly spectacular play by Maurie—

FULL SHOT—INT. ROYALS ARENA— NIGHT

A new automobile stands in the middle of the playing area. Beside it, A MAN stands at a microphone. In the background, the Royals team is seated on the bench. We can see, behind them, the stands filled with spectators—

CLOSER ANGLE—ON FLOOR

MAN AT MICROPHONE

. . . And so, it is my privilege to announce the player who has been selected by the sportswriters of the United States as the outstanding rookie of the year in the NBA . . . And I know that I speak for most of them when I say that this rookie may also be the outstanding *player* of the year . . .

Big Mo . . . Maurie Stokes of the Royals! . . . As the players on the bench join in the applause welling up from the spectators, Maurie rises and jogs up to the microphone. The man shakes Maurie's hand and hands him the keys to the car. As the applause dies down—

MAURIE

Thanks very much. I never expected anything like this. And I hope everybody realizes that this couldn't have happened without the help of all the guys on the team . . .

As the applause starts up again the man gestures to Maurie to drive the car off the floor. Maurie hesitates—

MAN AT MICROPHONE

It's all yours, Big Mo, drive it off.

MAURIE

You'd better clear the arena first.

MAN AT MICROPHONE *(puzzled)*

How's that?

MAURIE
I don't know how to drive . . .

As the crowd roars, Jack, grinning, leaps up from
the bench and joins Maurie at the car. Laughing,
Maurie and Jack get in the car and Jack drives
off the floor and down the ramp at the end of the
arena.

EXT. PARKING LOT BEHIND ARENA—
NIGHT

The parking lot is just about empty,—a last few
spectators driving off. Maurie and Jack, in street
clothes and each carrying a duffel bag, exit the
arena and approach Maurie's new car, parked in
solitary splendor.

CLOSE ANGLE—AT CAR

Maurie and Jack stop at the car and stare at it.

MAURIE
What the hell am I going to do with it?

JACK
Well, you can't leave it here. I'll drive you home.
Kick a tire and get in.

MAURIE
Kick a tire?

JACK
Getting in a new car without kicking a tire is un-
American.

LARGER ANGLE

They get into the car, Jack at the wheel, and drive
off.

EXT. A CINCINNATI STREET—NIGHT

It is a neighborhood of modest apartment houses.
Cars are parked, bumper to bumper, along the
curbs. Maurie's car comes slowly down the street.

CLOSE SHOT—INT. CAR

JACK   *(glancing around)*
. . . We're not going to find a place on the street
to put this thing.

MAURIE
Well, I can't take it apart and bring it upstairs
with me.

JACK   *(impatiently)*
Knock it off, Mo. You've got to find a place to
store this thing. Is there a garage near here?

MAURIE
How much does a garage cost?

JACK
By the month? About $45.

MAURIE   *(staring)*
You're joking!

JACK
Then why aren't you laughing?

MAURIE

My apartment doesn't cost much more than that. I'm not paying 45 a month for a car I can't even drive.

JACK

So you'll learn.

MAURIE

I've already learned not to spend money for something I don't need . . .

As they slowly drive, Maurie is looking around intently.

MAURIE *(pointing)*

Pull in here . . .

LARGER ANGLE

The car stops a few feet from the entrance to a used car lot.

INT. CAR

JACK *(incredulous)*

You're out of your mind!

MAURIE *(firmly)*

Pull in . . .

JACK *(aghast)*

You wouldn't! . . .

MAURIE

What's this thing worth new?

JACK

About 3500. But . . .

MAURIE *(firmly interrupts)*

In . . .

LARGER ANGLE

The car pulls into the lot and stops. The used car
dealer comes out of his little office shack and approaches the car.

CLOSE ANGLE—AT CAR

As the dealer looks the car over, deadpan, Maurie
gets out and approaches the dealer.

MAURIE

How much?

DEALER *(shrugging)*

Lemme look at the blue book . . .

He takes the book from his pocket and studies it.
His whole demeanor is one of negotiation. He is
the sort of used car dealer you wouldn't buy one
from and shouldn't sell one to. Jack gets out of
the car. The dealer puts the blue book in his
pocket and sighs expansively—

DEALER

Well, gentlemen . . . this is a pretty clean car.

MAURIE *(deadpan)*

Pretty clean? Not very clean?

DEALER *(broadly)*
How long does a car stay very clean?

JACK
Would you believe twenty minutes?

DEALER *(laughing mirthlessly)*
That's very funny . . .

(reeking with sincerity)
. . . I gotta be honest with ya, this is a pretty clean car. Mind starting the engine?

Jack reaches in and turns the engine over. The dealer listens with the intensity of Crosby listening to Sinatra. After a moment he purses his lips and nods.

DEALER
I gotta be honest with ya. It doesn't sound like it needs too much work.

MAURIE
I gotta be honest with ya . . . it doesn't need *any* work.

DEALER *(piously)*
Sir . . . I gotta be honest with ya . . . They don't build 'em the way they used to. But I gotta admit that I think I can get this thing looking and running like new.

JACK *(mock awe)*
That's hard to believe.

DEALER *(expertly)*

Well, we know how to do those things. What's the mileage on this?

MAURIE

Take a look . . .

The dealer sticks his head in and looks. Then he straightens up and smiles wisely.

DEALER

I gotta be honest with ya . . . we set the mileage back too sometimes. But lemme give you a tip . . .

(conspiratorially)

. . . you set this one back too much. Seven miles? You overdone it.

MAURIE

Really?

DEALER

Yeah. You shoulda left it at a couple of thousand.

MAURIE

How much?

DEALER

I can go . . . maybe 2800.

JACK

I could tell you where else you can go.

DEALER *(mirthlessly)*

Ha, ha. 29?

MAURIE
Keep going.

DEALER
Okay, 3000. And I'll stand the expense of getting this thing in shape.

MAURIE
Would you believe I haven't had a minute's trouble with it?

JACK
And he hasn't spent a nickel on it.

DEALER *(shaking head chidingly)*
You shouldn't neglect a car like that. I gotta be honest with ya. 3100's the best I can do.

JACK *(to Maurie)*
Let's go, Mo.

Jack starts to get into the car.

MAURIE *(to dealer)*
Can you write a check for 3200 before we drive out of here?

The dealer hesitates. Maurie starts to go around to get into the car.

DEALER
Okay, okay. 3200.

Jack gets out of the car.

DEALER *(in a low voice)*
But I gotta know something. This car hot?

MAURIE
Hot as a pistol.

DEALER
You got any registration?

MAURIE *(nods)*
And you can't tell it from the real thing.

He takes the registration slip from his pocket.

DEALER
Okay . . . I gotta be honest with ya. We just
keep this quiet, huh?

JACK *(piously)*
We won't tell a soul.

DEALER
Be with ya in a minute . . .

He walks toward the shack.

JACK *(to Maurie)*
What did you tell him it was hot for?

MAURIE *(shrugging)*
To make him happy. He'll get more pleasure sell-
ing a hot car than a cold one.

JACK *(sardonically)*
That was very considerate of you.

The dealer comes back with a checkbook, leans

over the hood and writes out a check. He hands the pen to Maurie.

DEALER
Sign the registration.

Maurie signs the slip and hands it to the dealer.

DEALER *(studying it)*
Maurice Stokes . . . that's a familiar name . . . like I heard it somewhere.

MAURIE
That's why I use it.

DEALER
Okay fellas, nice doin' business with ya. Anytime you get your hands on somethin' clean like this, lemme hear from ya.

JACK *(nods)*
I gotta be honest with ya . . . our next heist is yours.

As Maurie and Jack turn to leave, Maurie pats the fender of the car.

MAURIE *(to the car)*
I'll miss you pal . . .

LARGER ANGLE

As the dealer gets in the car and drives it to the back of the lot, Jack and Maurie walk from the lot and stop on the sidewalk.

CLOSE ANGLE—JACK & MAURIE

JACK   (broadly)

This is great! You're one block from home, and I'm nine miles from mine!

MAURIE   (mock sympathy)

Gee, that's tough. But I gotta be honest with ya . . . if I had a car I'd be glad to drive you home . . . Night . . .

He turns and starts up the block. Grinning and shaking his head, Jack looks off and waves his hand—

JACK   (calling out)

Taxi! . . .

DOROTHY'S   APARTMENT—KITCHEN—NIGHT

Maurie dries the last of some dishes, which Dorothy stows in a cupboard.

MAURIE

You're a dangerous woman . . .

DOROTHY

Dangerous? I thought it was a particularly good dinner.

MAURIE

That's what I mean . . .

They move into the living room—

INT. LIVING ROOM

DOROTHY *(not unkindly)*
What's bugging you, Maurie?

MAURIE
You.

DOROTHY
Gee, thanks.

MAURIE
If you were beautiful, that'd be great. Or if you were smart, that'd be very interesting. Or if you could cook up a storm, that'd be nice. But all three?

DOROTHY *(a little smile)*
Too much?

MAURIE
For me.

DOROTHY
Why?

MAURIE
'Cause a fellow has to take a girl like you seriously.

DOROTHY
Good.

MAURIE
Bad . . .

(a beat)
. . . Look, I don't want you to have any wrong ideas. If things were a little different . . .

DOROTHY

How different? . . . In 2 years you're an All-Star.

MAURIE

But I've still got a way to go to make sure. A guy gets hot for a year or two, and then he fades. I've got to work like hell for a few years to make sure it's going to last. To deserve the kind of money I need to take care of my folks. And to take care of a girl like you.

DOROTHY

You'll make it.

MAURIE

Maybe. But I've got to be sure . . .

(looks at watch)

. . . Sack time . . . game tomorrow . . .

Dorothy nods and moves with him to the door. They stop, very close together—

CLOSE TWO SHOT—AT DOOR

MAURIE

You understand?

DOROTHY *(nods)*

Yes . . .

He puts his arms around her and holds her closely against him. CAMERA MOVES SLOWLY into his face until his EYES FILL THE FRAME and we OVERLAP to—

CLOSE SHOT EYES—MAURIE—INT. AIR-
PLANE—NIGHT

As CAMERA PULLS BACK SLOWLY from the
eyes, Maurie's head still rests against the airplane
seat backrest. But now, his face reflects intense
distress, and is bathed in perspiration. He sits upright, obviously struggling against whatever it
is that is distressing him. He is breathing labori-
ously. A STEWARDESS—very petite and pretty
—comes by and stops—

STEWARDESS
Pardon me, sir . . . are you all right?

It is a very pronounced Southern accent—and it
awakens Richie, seated beside Maurie. As Maurie
merely nods, Richie grins—

RICHIE
Lemme guess . . . you're from Brooklyn.

STEWARDESS (grinning)
You're not even close . . . I'm from Mississippi.

RICHIE (mock-recoils)
Good Lord . . . do I have to sit in the back of
the plane?

STEWARDESS
Not unless you want to . . .

(she grins)
. . . You must have been asleep a long time.

As Richie grins back, he suddenly becomes aware

of Maurie's distress. Maurie is now leaning forward, his hands on the seat in front of him, breathing heavily.

RICHIE

What's goin' on, Mo?

Maurie doesn't reply. His distress is obviously mounting. As the Stewardess moves away quickly, several of the players seated nearby awaken and look toward Maurie—

EDDIE *(to Richie)*

With what you stowed away at the airport, *you're* the one should be sick . . .

RICHIE *(shrugging, perplexed)*

All he had was a sandwich and a glass of milk . . .

The Stewardess quickly returns into the shot and wipes Maurie's forehead with a cold wet cloth—

STEWARDESS

Try to relax, sir . . . you'll be all right . . .

Maurie responds with a very weak, strained smile of appreciation and rests his head back against the seat. The Stewardess wipes the perspiration from his face, smiles comfortingly and moves off. For just an instant, Maurie rests against the seat and then begins to shake, uncontrollably. He sits upright. As his face contorts, with a great effort he rises to his feet. As Jack, now concerned, starts to rise to move toward him, Maurie pitches forward and collapses in the aisle of the plane. Jack and several players squeeze into the narrow aisle beside Maurie's prostrate body. His eyes are closed now and he is breathing with great difficulty. The first Stewardess forces her way to Maurie, a SEC-OND STEWARDESS behind her—

> FIRST STEWARDESS (*quickly*)
> Oxygen!

Maurie is partly on his side. With an effort, the Stewardess and a couple of the players turn his massive body on to his back. The second Stewardess quickly reaches up to the overhead rack, unfastens the oxygen container and starts to hand it to the first Stewardess, who is examining Maurie closely—

> FIRST STEWARDESS (*hastily, shaking head*)
> He's not breathing! . . . Tell the Captain to radio ahead for an ambulance! . . .

She obviously knows what she is doing. She straddles Maurie, leans forward and starts to give him mouth-to-mouth resuscitation. As the players watch, stunned,—the second Stewardess and the FIRST OFFICER appear—

> FIRST OFFICER
> There'll be an ambulance waiting in Cincinnati . . . we'll be there in ten minutes . . .

> JACK
> Anything we can do?

FIRST OFFICER

She's doing it . . .

With a steady, relentless rhythm, the Stewardess forces air into Maurie's slack mouth.

INTERIOR HOSPITAL. CLOSE SHOT—MAURIE—TREATMENT ROOM—DAY

The massive body of Maurie is stretched out on a large table. It is completely encased in plastic ice-filled containers,—an oxygen mask over his mouth and nose. An ATTENDANT is replacing melted containers with ones containing fresh ice. CAMERA PULLS BACK to reveal Jack and DOCTOR STEWART. Jack watches, stunned—

JACK

What is it?

DR. STEWART

We thought it was encephalitis. But tests for that are negative. Now we're exploring the possibility of a brain injury. Did he have an accident? A fall?

JACK

We all fall sometimes. But I don't remember Maurie really being injured. He took a spill and bumped his head last week. But it wasn't serious . . . He kept on playing.

DR. STEWART

There is often a delayed reaction to a head injury. This could be a traumatic encethalopathy.

JACK

What's going to happen?

DR. STEWART

We're doing everything we can to bring him out of this coma.

JACK

He'll make it, won't he?

DR. STEWART

He's a rugged fellow. That will help. Does he have any family?

JACK

I think his folks live in Pittsburgh.

DR. STEWART

Somebody better notify them.

Jack nods and as they start out of the treatment room—

DR. STEWART

Would you step in my office a moment, please . . .

INT. DR. STEWART'S OFFICE

As Jack, troubled, stands there, Dr. Stewart takes some things from a manila envelope—

DR. STEWART

These are Mr. Stokes' personal effects. Would you wish to take care of them for him?

JACK

Sure . . .

DR. STEWART *(handing Jack a paper)*
Please sign here . . .

JACK *(signing paper)*
May I use your phone?

DR. STEWART
Of course . . .

He exits the office. Deeply troubled, Jack looks at the contents of the manila envelope—a wristwatch, a wallet, a ring, etc. There is also a small velvet box. Jack opens the box. It contains a diamond ring. For just an instant, troubled and perplexed, Jack fingers the effects, particularly the ring. He picks up the phone and dials—

JACK *(on phone)*
. . . Honey? . . . I'm still at the hospital . . . No . . . Doesn't look good . . . You'd better go ahead . . . I'll be a little late . . .

He hangs up the phone,—and then picks it up again. He dials Operator—

JACK
. . . Operator? . . . Would you please get me information in Pittsburgh? . . .

RECEPTION AREA—NEAR ELEVATOR—
HOSPITAL—DAY

In the Reception Area, Dr. Stewart stands talking to Mr. and Mrs. Stokes. The elevator door opens and, as Jack exits, Dr. Stewart leaves the Stokes and moves toward Jack.

CLOSE ANGLE   JACK & DR. STEWART

JACK

Thanks for calling me. How'd they take it?

DR. STEWART

Hard.

JACK

Figured.

DR. STEWART

But they're solid. That helps.

JACK

How is he?

DR. STEWART

No change yet.

As Dr. Stewart moves down the corridor, Jack moves into the Reception Area toward the Stokes.

CLOSER ANGLE—RECEPTION AREA

Mr. Stokes' arm is around Mrs. Stokes' shoulder as they stand, waiting,—solidly resisting this staggering blow. Somehow, they manage to control the agonizing apprehension they feel . . .

JACK

I'm Jack Twyman.

Silently, they shake hands.

MR. STOKES

We appreciate your calling us . . .

JACK

Have you seen Maurie? . . .

(they nod sadly)

. . . I . . . I'm sorry . . .

MRS. STOKES

The doctor explained it to us. Is Maurie going to die?

JACK *(struggling)*

I . . . I just don't know . . .

MR. STOKES

Could we talk to you?

JACK

Of course . . .

He gestures them toward one of the sofas,—and sits facing them. Mrs. Stokes sits tensely, Mr. Stokes is hunched forward, arms resting on his knees. He looks up at Jack—

MR. STOKES

We've never been faced with anything like this.

JACK

I know. It's rough.

MR. STOKES

The doctor says Maurie can't be moved. And we can't keep coming back and forth from Pittsburgh. I can't afford it. 'Specially now. With my job and all. But Maurie's got to be taken good care of.

JACK *(reassuringly)*

He will be.

MR. STOKES

We've got to be sure.

JACK

I know you can't stay here. But I live in Cincinnati. I'd be glad to check on how things go and let you know.

MRS. STOKES

We don't mean to burden you.

JACK

It'd be no problem. Meantime, try not to worry.

MR. STOKES *(quietly firm)*

We'll worry . . . but we won't come apart.

JACK *(a reassuring smile)*

Good. And I'll keep in touch with you.

Mrs. Stokes looks at Jack for just a beat, and when she speaks it is with an utterly simple and ingenuous sincerity—

MRS. STOKES

That is very nice of you.

As they rise—

JACK

May I drive you to the airport?

> MR. STOKES

We'll take the bus back to Pittsburgh. No point in squandering . . .

> JACK

I'll drive you to the depot . . .

As they move off toward the elevator—

INT. TWYMAN HOUSE—BABY'S ROOM— NIGHT

It is late. In a robe, hair tousled, eyes sleepy, Carole sits beside the crib. Lisa, about 8 months old, is in Carole's arms feeding from a bottle. They finish and Carole gently places Lisa back in her crib and tucks the covers around her. Then she picks up an alarm clock standing on a table beside the crib and, as she moves toward the adjoining bedroom, she re-sets the alarm—

INT. TWYMAN BEDROOM—NIGHT

Except for faint light coming in through the sliding doors to the backyard, the room is in darkness. Groggily, Carole places the clock on her night-table, takes off her robe and starts to get into bed which, in disarray, has obviously been slept in. But before she can settle down, she notices that Jack is not there. Somewhat surprised, she rises and puts on her robe as she moves toward the sliding door to the backyard—

MEDIUM SHOT—BACKYARD

In a robe, deeply preoccupied, Jack is seated on a

chaise. In the background, Carole moves slowly toward him.

CLOSE ANGLE—AT CHAISE

She sits beside him. For a long moment they are silent.

> JACK *(finally)*
> I don't know what the hell to do.

> CAROLE
> Maurie?

> JACK *(nodding)*
> You know that bank book I found in his apartment? Well, he's got over $8,000 in a bank here in Cincinnati . . .

> CAROLE
> That should pay a lot of bills . . .

> JACK
> But we can't get at the money. Only Maurie can do that.

> CAROLE
> Couldn't the money be turned over to his folks?

> JACK
> I suppose so. But that'd mean lawyers, court proceedings . . . and it wouldn't be easy for them to handle things back there in Pittsburgh. Mr. Stokes works in the steel mill . . . they've got all they can do to keep themselves going as it is.

CAROLE

This could go on for quite a while, couldn't it?

JACK *(nods)*

Mo doesn't give up easily . . .

(a beat)

. . . I'll call his folks tomorrow.

They rise and, arms around each other, move slowly back toward the bedroom—

INT. BEDROOM

As they enter—

CAROLE

You never said much about Maurie. What kind of fellow was he?

JACK

A good guy . . .

They remove their robes and get into bed. Reflectively, Jack lies on his back, eyes open. On her side, Carole studies him for a moment. Then she leans over and kisses him—

CAROLE

So are you . . .

EXT. BUS TERMINAL—DAY

Mr. Stokes is sitting on a bench outside the terminal as Jack's car pulls up and stops. As Jack gets out, Mr. Stokes moves toward him and they shake hands—

CLOSE TWO SHOT—AT CAR

MR. STOKES

I didn't mean to inconvenience you . . . but I'd like to talk.

JACK

Sure . . .

He opens the car door for Mr. Stokes and they get in.

INT. CAR

It is obvious that Mr. Stokes has thought long and hard—

MR. STOKES

Mrs. Stokes and me have talked this all out. And we decided there was only one thing to do. Maurie has got to be taken good care of. And it's up to us to do it. We mortgaged the house . . .

(he takes check from pocket)

. . . $9,000. That oughta take care of anything he needs.

JACK

But what about you? That's a big debt to assume.

MR. STOKES *(nods)*

Maybe. But there's no other way. We talked about pulling up stakes and moving here, so we could be near Maurie. But it wouldn't do no good. At my time of life, what kind of job could I get? I been in that mill in Pittsburgh over thirty years.

And now's no time to be walkin' away from it. It ain't much, but it's sure. And Mrs. Stokes is gonna do all she can. That's why she didn't come today. She's doin' some part-time work . . .

He sits for a moment and then looks at Jack, with a firm quiet pride.

MR. STOKES

We can do what needs to be done.

Jack is deeply moved by the simple, resolute way in which these people have confronted their enormous burden.

JACK

Is there any way I can help you?

MR. STOKES *(forthrightly)*

Mr. Twyman . . . I was hopin' you'd ask that. Would you look after this money for us and pay what's got to be paid?

JACK

Of course.

Mr. Stokes hands him the check.

JACK

Mr. Stokes . . . I hope you don't mind my asking . . . but what about that money Maurie's got in the bank?

MR. STOKES

We talked about that. And we don't want to touch

it. If Maurie comes out of this, it'll be a while
'fore he's able to do for himself. And it might help
him if he know he's got something to fall back on.

JACK

But he might not want you to take on all the burden yourself.

MR. STOKES

We always shared . . . good and bad. This is the
right way . . .

(a beat)

. . . There's a bus back to Pittsburgh in a little
while. But I'd like to see Maurie first . . .

Jack nods and starts the car.

LARGER ANGLE

As the car drives off.

INT. HOSPITAL—BUSINESS OFFICE—DAY

Jack is seated at a desk with the hospital administrator.

ADMINISTRATOR

. . . And we'll render you an itemized accounting
each week.

JACK *(nodding)*

Do you think this will cover everything that's
needed?

ADMINISTRATOR

That's impossible to tell—until they manage to

pinpoint the precise injury—the first thing is to bring him out of his coma . . .

His phone rings and he answers it—

ADMINISTRATOR

. . . Hello? . . . Yes . . . Yes, I'll tell him . . .

(hangs up)

. . . That was Dr. Stewart. Maurie has a visitor and he thought you might want to see her.

JACK   *(rising)*

Thank you . . .

As he exits—

ANGLE FROM NURSES STATION—TOWARD ENTRANCE DOOR

A nurse is behind station counter as Jack comes through the door and moves to the station.

JACK

Mr. Stokes has a visitor?

NURSE   *(nods)*

She's in there with him now . . .

Jack turns away from station and starts down the right-hand corridor. After a couple of steps, he slows and stops. He waits in the corridor. Over him, the door to Maurie's room, a short way down the corridor, is open. As he stands there, a male attendant goes by him his arms laden with ice-filled plastic bags. The attendant goes into Maurie's room. A moment later, Dorothy backs slowly out of the room. She stands for just a beat, looking back into the room, and then turns and, clearly distraught, moves slowly up the corridor toward Jack.

DOROTHY

Mr. Twyman . . . I'm Dorothy Parsons, from New York . . .

JACK   *(shaking hands)*

Hi . . . I could use a cup of coffee . . . how about you?

Dorothy nods, and they move toward patio.

ANGLE ON PATIO—DAY

Jack and Dorothy come out on to the patio and sit at one of the tables. They are silent for a moment, Jack compassionately studying a desolate Dorothy.

DOROTHY

. . . To see him lying there . . . like that. . . he's barely alive . . .

JACK

But he *is.*

DOROTHY

How long can this go on?

JACK

No one knows. But they're doing everything they can.

DOROTHY

It seems terrible to think of things like this now
. . . but . . . who's going to take care of all this?
It must be costing a fortune.

JACK

Maurie's parents have bitten the bullet. They're
extraordinary people.

DOROTHY   *(nods)*
Yes.

JACK

You know them?

DOROTHY   *(shaking head)*
But I know Maurie.

Jack studies her for a moment, as a nurse puts 2
cups of coffee on the table, and then he smiles—

JACK

I'm amazed at Mo.

DOROTHY   *(a little surprised)*
Why?

JACK   *(grins)*
You've never been in a locker room, have you?

DOROTHY   *(a little grin)*
Hardly . . .

JACK

You wouldn't believe some of the dialogue. Sometimes it sounds like a convention of Casanovas.

DOROTHY

The locker room must be more fascinating than the games.

JACK *(chuckling)*

If only 10% of that talk was on the level, those guys couldn't even crawl out to the court.

DOROTHY

But why are you amazed at Maurie?

JACK

That he could have a girl like you and not boast about it.

DOROTHY

That's a nice compliment . . . for Maurie.

JACK

It was meant to be for you.

DOROTHY *(a small smile)*

Has it ever occurred to you that he might have some other girls to boast about . . .

(a little grimace)

. . . The thought has occurred to me.

JACK

Are you going to stay here for a while?

DOROTHY *(soberly)*

I would, if there were something I could do . . . if he just knew I was here . . .

JACK

You have a job in New York?

(Dorothy nods)

I'll be on the road with the team for about a week.
When I get back I'd be glad to call and let you
know if there's any change.

She studies him appreciatively for a moment.

DOROTHY

I guess we're even.

JACK   *(puzzled)*

Even?

DOROTHY   *(nods)*

Mo didn't boast about you either . . .

INT. HOSPITAL—DESK & RECEPTION
AREA—MAURIE'S FLOOR—NIGHT

Jack exits the elevator, carrying a suitcase. He puts
it down beside the desk and moves toward the door
to Maurie's room. The desk nurse comes out from
behind the desk and joins Jack—

DESK NURSE

Mr. Twyman . . . Dr. Stewart left word that he
wanted to see you as soon as you got back.

JACK

It's after midnight . . .

DESK NURSE

How about eight tomorrow morning?

JACK

Okay . . .

He enters Maurie's room.

MEDIUM SHOT—INT. MAURIE'S ROOM

The room is quite dark. There is a dim light coming from a lamp on the bureau. But even in the dim light, we can see that Maurie is no longer on the double table, encased in ice packs. He is in a regulation bed, covered with a sheet. He is not using oxygen. His arms are half-crossed on his stomach. Jack moves quietly to the side of the bed and peers down at Maurie, whose head is in shadow.

Something that Jack sees startles him. His hand moves quickly to the bed lamp and turns it on. It shines directly on Maurie's face,—and we can see that Maurie's eyes are wide open and staring at Jack. For just an instant, Jack reflects surprise, almost shock,—and then a smile of relief plays across his face—

JACK

Hi . . .

Maurie just stares at him. Not a muscle moves. His lips, slightly open, are inert. But the eyes seem to be alert, though unblinking. Jack studies him for a moment—

JACK

Can you hear me?

For just an instant, Maurie is totally unresponsive. Then his eyes blink once—

JACK
Does that blink mean anything?

Maurie blinks his eyes two or three times—

JACK
Okay, let's get squared away. If you can hear and understand what I'm saying . . . blink once . . .
(Maurie blinks once)

. . . If you can't say anything to me, blink twice . . .
(Maurie blinks twice)

. . . You are a member of the Boston Celtics . . .
(Maurie blinks twice)

. . . The Cincinnati Royals? . . .
(Maurie blinks once)

. . . Then you can hear and understand everything I'm saying? . . .
(Maurie blinks once)

. . . I'm the greatest basketball player who ever lived . . .
(Maurie blinks twice)

. . . You're the greatest basketball player who ever lived . . .
(Maurie blinks once)

. . . You are also the most conceited basketball player who ever lived . . .

...aurie blinks once. Then, incredibly, an almost
guttural chuckle emerges from lips which move
slightly, in a vague version of a smile. Jack stares
at him, puzzled—

                    JACK
Can you say *anything?*

Maurie's face is back to its inert, impassive expression. But he blinks twice. Jack stares at him soberly
for just a moment, and then he breathes an exaggerated sigh—

                    JACK
Well, this isn't the most sparkling conversation
I've ever had. I'll see you in the morning. Try to
stay awake 'til I get back, okay?

Maurie blinks once and there is an almost imper-
ceptible suggestion of a smile on his lips. It is
minimal.

                    JACK   (casually)
Good night, pal . . .

As he exits the room, the CAMERA MOVES
INTO VERY CLOSE SHOT—MAURIE'S FACE

As he lies there totally impassive and immobile.
But the eyes are wide, alert and fully reflective of
the thoughts going on behind them.

INT. DR. STEWART'S OFFICE—DAY

Jack is pacing the floor, obviously highly arous
by his visit with Maurie the night before—

JACK

. . . But he seemed to understand everything I
said!

DR. STEWART

His mind is as clear as a bell. But, Jack, that's the
only thing that's functioning. The injury affected
that part of the brain which controls the voluntary
action of the rest of the muscles of the body. He has
no control of them whatsoever.

JACK

He must have *some* control. I got off a weak joke
last night . . . and he smiled. I could see it. His
lips moved a little.

DR. STEWART *(nodding)*

I know. After he regained consciousness, we were
making some tests. One of the technicians made a
joke and Maurie reacted slightly. And we realized
that Genuine laughter is a totally reflex action.
Like breathing. But except for his eyelids, it's liter-
ally impossible for him to do anything voluntarily.
He hears and understands and if you say something
funny he will react a little, spontaneously. But he
couldn't make himself smile politely even if his
life depended on it.

Jack stops pacing. His spirited eagerness has been
badly dampened by this analysis.

JACK

Isn't there something you can do to restore his voluntary movement and actions?

DR. STEWART

Every muscle in his body would have to be taught to function, as if he had never had use of them in his life.

JACK *(earnestly)*

But it could be done?

DR. STEWART

Theoretically . . .

(a somber pause)

. . . Jack, we might as well face it. The kind of therapy that is theoretically possible would be arduous, tedious, and it would take years. Frankly, I think it would be beyond the spiritual and physical resources of even a magnificent specimen like Maurie. And the second problem would be the cost. Therapists for every function of his body. Years of it. It's almost inconceivable that any human could carry such a sustained, relentless burden . . . spiritually, physically and financially.

JACK

What *would* it cost?

DR. STEWART

My guess is that it would be close to $100,000 a year.

For a long moment, Jack digests this somberly—

JACK   *(quietly)*

Let's get started . . .

DR. STEWART   *(pointedly)*

Jack . . . some arrangements would have to be made.

JACK

How much is left of that $9,000 on his account?

DR. STEWART

About $3,000.

JACK

Okay . . . that's for starters.

DR. STEWART   *(dubiously)*

You know how long that will last?

JACK

By then I'll figure something out.

DR. STEWART

We'd have to move him to Dr. Walker's therapy section in the North Wing.

JACK

Okay, let's move him.

INT. MAURIE'S ROOM—DAY

Present are Dr. Stewart, Jack and two male attendants. Maurie is stretched out on the bed,— naked except for a pair of jockey shorts. Beside the bed is a rolling table stretcher. Dr. Stewart and the attendants are attaching heavy braces to

aurie's legs and torso. He lies there, inert, star-
ng up at Jack.

JACK
We're moving you to the North Wing . . .

Maurie blinks his eyes five or six times, fast.

JACK
You want to know *why* we're moving you? . . .
(Maurie blinks once)

. . . Because the nurses in the North Wing are
dolls. And I haven't been getting anywhere with
the nurses in the South Wing.

A strained, muffled chortle from Maurie. By now,
his entire body, from feet to shoulders, is strapped
into the braces. One of the attendants crosses
Maurie's arms atop his torso. The other attendant
opens Maurie's mouth with his fingers, reaches in
and inserts a thick wad of gauze.

JACK
What's that for?

DR. STEWART
So he won't swallow his tongue.

JACK   *(mock-scoffing)*
No chance of that. He's fussy about what he
eats . . .

The four men take hold of Maurie's huge frame

and lift him from the bed on to the rolling tab.
They cover him with a sheet and roll him out o
the room.

INT. MAURIE'S ROOM—NORTH WING— NIGHT

The rolling stretcher is beside the bed. Jack and
the two male attendants are lifting the braced figure of Maurie from the stretcher table to the
bed. Just as they do, NURSE ROSIE SANDERS
enters. She is a short, rotund woman who exudes
energy and joviality. And when she smiles or
laughs—as she does often—her glistening white
teeth, projecting from her dark face, light up the
room. As the two male attendants unstrap the
braces from Maurie's body—

> ROSIE   *(to Jack)*
I guess you're Mr. Twyman . . . I'm Rosie Sanders.

> JACK   *(shaking hands)*
Nice to know you, Nurse Sanders.

> ROSIE
You going to be around much?

> JACK
Some.

> ROSIE
Then start calling me Rosie . . .

She moves beside the bed and looks Maurie over
from head to toe—

ROSIE *(ebbulliently)*
My, my! You're a big one, aren't you?

Maurie blinks his eyes several times.

ROSIE *(broadly chiding)*
Don't blink those flirty eyes at me. I'm old enough to be your mother.

JACK *(drily)*
The shape he's in, he'll take whatever he can get.

A laugh gurgles from Maurie. The two attendants have unfastened all of the braces and exit the room. As Rosie covers Maurie with a sheet and adjusts his bed, Jack moves close to Maurie and looks down at him—

JACK
Is there anything you want? . . .
(Maurie blinks once)

. . . Is the first letter before 'M'? . . .
(Maurie blinks twice)

After 'M' . . . N-O-P-Q-R-S-T-U-V . . .

Maurie stares unblinking as Jack goes through the letters. At 'W' he blinks once.

JACK
'W' . . . is the second letter before 'M'? . . .

(Maurie blinks once)
. . . 'A'? . . .

(Maurie blinks once)

. . . 'W-A' . . . is the third letter before 'M'? . . .
(Maurie blinks twice)

. . . M-N-O-P-Q-R-S . . .
        At 'T' Maurie blinks once.

. . . 'W-A-T' . . . water?

Maurie blinks once. As Jack reaches for a glass of
water beside the bed—

ROSIE   *(impressed)*
That's pretty good . . . let me do that . . .

She picks up a spoon and takes a spoonful of water
from the glass. With the fingers of her left hand,
she opens Maurice's lips and, with no resistance, is
able to part his teeth. She puts two fingers into
his mouth to depress his tongue and then inserts
the spoon over the fingers and drops the water
into his mouth. Almost instantaneously we can see
Maurie's larynx react as he swallows—

JACK   *(surprised)*
I thought he couldn't do anything voluntarily.

ROSIE
He can't. But when something gets in his throat
the swallowing is reflex . . .

As she reaches for another spoonful of water—

JACK

Giving him a drink that way'll take all day. Hold it a minute . . .

There are some straws in a container on the service table. He selects one, puts it in the glass of water and sucks the water up until it fills the straw.

Then, at the same instant he takes the straw from his lips, he presses his forefinger against the upper end of the straw,—retaining the water in the straw. Then he pries Maurie's mouth open with the fingers of his left hand and inserts the straw deeply into Maurie's mouth. He then releases his finger from the top of the straw, and we can see Maurie's larynx bob several times as he swallows the descending stream of water from the straw in his mouth.

ROSIE *(staring)*

Just like siphoning gas from a car!

JACK *(grinning)*

Oh, you had a misspent youth, too, huh?

Chuckling, Rosie starts to arrange some of the supplies on the table beside the bed, as Jack continues to siphon water into Maurie's mouth.

INT. TWYMAN BEDROOM—NIGHT

The room is in darkness as Jack, in payjamas, exits from the bathroom. A reflection of light from the outside casts a faint glow over the bed in which Carole is asleep on her side. Quietly, Jack

slides into the bed beside her. And he lies there
for a long moment, hands clasped behind his head,
his eyes troubled. Then, he looks toward Carole—

JACK   *(in a soft whisper)*

Honey . . .

Drowsily, Carole rolls on to her other side, facing
Jack. Without opening her eyes, she sleepily extends one arm and lays it across Jack's chest.

CAROLE   *(almost inaudibly)*

Mmm? . . .

JACK   *(in a whisper)*

Are you asleep?

CAROLE   *(groggily, eyes half-open)*

Not any more . . .

Jack eases on to his side, facing her. He places his
right hand on her shoulder and caresses it tenderly, as they lie close together.

JACK

You really awake?

With an exaggerated effort she forces her eyes
wide open.

CAROLE   *(sleepily)*

Sure. What time is it?

JACK

After two.

CAROLE

Late. What happened?

JACK

There was a lot to do . . . getting him settled
. . . making arrangements . . .

CAROLE

Everything all right?

JACK

I guess . . .

CAROLE *(snuggling closer)*
You'd better get some sleep.

JACK *(after a beat)*

Honey?

CAROLE

Mmm? . . .

JACK

What would you think about an addition to the
family?

Her eyes really open now as she stares at him. And
a slight, almost coy smile plays across her face.
She kisses the tip of his nose.

CAROLE

Have you forgotten? We'll have one in a few
months.

JACK

How about another one?

CAROLE   *(a little grin)*

Isn't your timing a little off?

And then she notices that Jack is not responding in kind to her light, amused response. She looks at him questioningly—

CAROLE   *(teasing)*

Are you making a pass or aren't you?

JACK

Well . . . sort of . . .

CAROLE

You said something about an addition to the family . . .

JACK

Uh huh . . .

CAROLE   *(drily quizzical)*

What did you have in mind?

JACK

Maurie . . .

She stares at him,—wide-eyed and thoroughly awake.

EXT. STOKES HOME—PITTSBURGH—DAY

A taxi pulls up and stops. Jack gets out, pays the driver, moves to the front door, and rings the bell. A moment later Mrs. Stokes opens the door.

MRS. STOKES

Oh, Mr. Twyman . . . it's nice to see you . . .

As Jack enters—

INT. STOKES LIVING ROOM

Mr. Stokes comes into the room from the rear of
the house.

> MR. STOKES

How are you, Mr. Twyman?

He extends his hand. As Jack takes it—

> JACK   *(a little smile)*

I'm fine . . . and I'd be even better if you'd call
me Jack.

> MRS. STOKES

We sure appreciate your coming to see us. And all
your phone calls about Maurie.

> MR. STOKES

It's meant a lot to us.

> JACK

I thought it was time we had a little talk . . .
and not on the telephone . . .

> *(a beat)*

. . . Maurie is in for a long siege at that hospital.
Bringing him back is going to take a lot of time
and money.

> MR. STOKES   *(quietly)*

We've handled it this far. And I guess, some way,
we'll do what has to be done.

JACK   *(shakes head)*

I'm afraid not. To do what needs to be done will
cost almost $100,000 a year.

Mr. and Mrs. Stokes stare at Jack, shaken to the
core. Clearly, they had never envisioned anything
of such an enormous scale.

JACK

That's why I wanted to see you. Please don't be
offended. But I don't see how you can cope with
this sort of thing . . .

A silent beat as the Stokes try to digest this over-
whelming news.

JACK *(forthrightly)*

There's $3,000 left from your mortgage money.
That won't last a month. And Maurie has $8,000
in the bank . . . another couple of months.

MRS. STOKES

And then what?

JACK

That's what I want to talk about. Somehow money
will have to be raised. For a long time. Can you
do that?

MR. STOKES

Jack . . . I'd give my life if I could say that I could
. . . that *we* could. But we can't. I guess you know
that. Who could?

JACK   *(simply)*

I'd like to try.

MRS. STOKES

You? How?

JACK

Well, first of all, we have to get that money out of Maurie's bank account. And then additional funds will have to be raised and decisions made for Maurie. I realize that you can't move to Cincinnati. But I live there. And if you would agree, I think the best way is for me to go to court . . . and become Maurie's guardian.

MRS. STOKES   (wide-eyed)

You mean, *adopt* Maurie?

JACK

Well, I guess you could put it that way. And then . . . just do the best I can.

There is a long moment as the Stokes study Jack, deeply moved by his extraordinary suggestion.

MR. STOKES   (pointedly)

Why?

JACK

Why what?

MR. STOKES

Why would you offer to do a thing like that? Near as I can figure, you 'n Maurie weren't close friends . . .

JACK

We were teammates . . .

MR. STOKES

. . . But teammates and friends are different.
What you're talking about is . . . well . . . you
got a family?

JACK *(nods)*

A wife . . . and one and half children . . .

(a little smile)

. . . We're having our second in a few months.

MR. STOKES *(not impolitely)*

You a rich man?

JACK *(smiling)*

I got a $3,000 raise this year. And we celebrated
for two days. That answer your question?

MR. STOKES

I figured that. Seems to me you got all you can do
to take care of your own . . .

(very firmly)

. . . I want you to tell me why you would offer
to take on something like this?

JACK

Because I can't think of any other way . . .

(a beat)

. . . We got a deal?

Mr. Stokes studies Jack intently and then, silently,
offers his hand. Jack takes it and then turns
and offers his hand to Mrs. Stokes. But she just

moves to him, eyes brimming, reaches up, and kisses his check.

                    JACK
I'll be in touch . . .

He turns and leaves the house.

INT. PHYSICAL THERAPY ROOM—DAY

As Jack and Dr. Walker enter, two attendants are transferring Maurie, naked except for shorts, from a rolling table to a therapy table. The room is filled with equipment—pulleys extending from the ceiling, horizontal and vertical contraptions, two therapeutic tanks, etc.

Jack and Dr. Walker approach Maurie.

                 DR. WALKER
Good afternoon, Maurice, I'm Dr. Walker . . .

Maurie blinks several times.

                    JACK
Hi, Mo . . . he's your coach now, okay? . . .
            (Maurie blinks once)

. . . I just came from two hours of practice. Now it's your turn.

                 DR. WALKER
Maurie . . . we're going to put you through some exercises, to tone your muscles up. But we can't accomplish much unless you help us. I want you to understand one thing clearly. There is nothing

wrong with any of your muscles. There is also
nothing wrong with your brain . . .

> JACK   *(interrupting)*
> What he means, Mo, is . . . your brain's no worse
> now than it was before. How good it was then,
> who knows?

A little chuckle emerges from Maurie, and Dr.
Walker smiles.

> DR. WALKER   *(to Maurie)*
> He's a very brave guy . . . as long as *you* can't
> move . . .
>
>   *(he resumes, seriously)*
> . . . Our problem is to re-establish a connection
> between your brain and your muscles. It's as if you
> have forgotten how to make yourself move. You
> know how it is when you try to remember some-
> body's name? Or something that happened in the
> past? You think hard, trying to restore that piece
> of information. Now, what we're going to try to do
> is help you remember how to move. Do you under-
> stand that? . . .
>   *(Maurie blinks once)*
>
> . . . It's going to take a long time. And it's going
> to hurt. Are you ready for that?

Maurie blinks once, and Dr. Walker nods to the
attendants—

> DR. WALKER
> Okay . . .

.he first attendant places one hand on Maurie's chest and the other hand on Maurie's right knee. The second attendant flexes Maurie's left leg, raising the knee and then, gently, pushes Maurie's knee up and back toward his chest. There is no reaction from Maurie. And the attendant straightens the leg out. He repeats the flexing, this time a little further. This is repeated several times, each progressively harder and further. The fifth time he pushes Maurice's massive leg very hard, trying to push it against Maurie's chest. And suddenly Maurie grimaces in pain. As the attendant releases the leg—

DR. WALKER

Good. That hurt, didn't it?

Maurie, again in repose, blinks once.

DR. WALKER

We're going to keep doing that, with every part of your body, trying to induce the pain you felt. Because when you feel that pain you instinctively react against it. You don't have to will your reaction. Like when your hand touches a hot stove You pull it away without thinking. And as we continue to do this, and you instinctively react, the communication between your brain and your muscles will gradually restore.

He reaches down and takes Maurie's limp hand. With his fingers, Dr. Walker flexes Maurie's forefinger back and forth. The finger is limp and inert.

DR. WALKER

You can't move your finger, can you? . . .
(Maurice blinks twice)

. . . Try . . .

Maurie's limp hand lies in Dr. Walker's. Maurie
stares at his hand concentratedly,—and we can see
that he is trying to do something. But the finger lies there, inert. Dr. Walker pulls Maurie's
forefinger back a little. Then a little further. And
further. Suddenly, Maurie grimaces in pain. Dr.
Walker holds the finger at its painful angle—

DR. WALKER

There . . . that hurts . . . and your finger is instinctively trying to avoid the pain by pushing it-
self forward. I can feel the pressure . . .

He releases the finger and Maurie's expression of
pain disappears.

DR. WALKER

Eventually, if we all do our job, you should be
able to do these things voluntarily again. As I told
you, this is going to be a long and painful process.
If, at any time, it's too much for you, just start
blinking your eyes, and they'll stop and give you
some relief. Okay?

Maurie blinks once. The doctor nods toward the
attendants and exits the room. The two attendants
resume the rhythmic, intensely pressured flexing
of Maurie's legs. And each time they press Maurie's

leg into an extremely contracted position, his face reacts to the pain. Jack stands off to one side, watching. Perspiration begins to bead on Maurie's face. Rosie rinses out a damp cloth and bathes his face as he lies there,—his face alternating between expressionless repose and intense pain.

CLOSE HEAD SHOT—MAURIE

As his face reflects the rhythmically recurring pain, his eyes are wide open and he does not blink.

CLOSE SHOT—JACK

As he watches, out of the line of Maurie's vision, Jack's own eyes reflect, to some measure, the pain that he is witnessing. And there is torment in his expression as he realizes the course upon which he has helped Maurie to embark.

INT. MAURIE'S ROOM—DAY

Maurie is stretched out on the bed, covered with a towel, but otherwise naked. Jack stands beside the bed, as Rosie bathes and massages Maurie.

JACK
. . . They gave you a pretty good workout, didn't they?

Maurie blinks once. Jack nods toward the television set on the opposite wall.

JACK
You going to watch the game tonight?

Maurie blinks once. Jack looks disgruntled—

JACK

Sure . . . that figured. You'll lie there on your
butt, taking it easy, while we're breaking ours . . .

(to Rosie)

. . . How about coming over to the locker room
after the game and giving *me* a massage?

Rosie chuckles as she continues massaging
Maurie—

ROSIE

You break your butt, and I might just do that . . .

(a muffled laugh from Maurie)

. . . What are you laughing at? That'd be nice
duty. All those big, handsome fellows in the locker
room.

JACK

You're a dirty old woman.

ROSIE *(chuckling)*

I'm not so old . . .

The door opens and MISS HARRIS enters. She
is a slim, rather attractive gal in her thirties,—
wearing a white technician's jacket.

MISS HARRIS

I'm Miss Harris . . . your speech therapist.

JACK *(to Maurie)*

When you watch the game tonight . . . if the pic-

ture isn't clear, I'm the guy scoring all the points
and looking great.

ROSIE

You don't have to score any points . . . We'll
know who you are by your big head.

As Maurie chortles, Jack smiles and exits the room.
Rosie has finished bathing Maurie and has covered
him with a sheet. As she rolls the head of the bed
up to put Maurie in a semi-vertical position, Miss
Harris sits beside the bed, close to Maurie. She
opens a bottle of ointment and, as she rubs it
around Maurie's lips and face—

MISS HARRIS

Maurie, the first thing we're going to try to get
you to do is exhale . . .

With her fingers, she parts Maurie's lips. And
holds a finger close to them—

MISS HARRIS

Try to blow on my finger . . .

Maurie lies there, just breathing regularly.

MISS HARRIS

Don't be discouraged . . . just keep trying . . .

There is no visible change in Maurie's breathing
pattern. Miss Harris opens a box of matches, takes
one out and lights it. She holds it vertically, a few
inches from Maurie's lips.

MISS HARRIS
Try to blow it out . . .

There is no visible response from Maurie. She moves the lighted match closer to his lips. Closer. A little closer. There is a slight spontaneous flexing of his lips. She withdraws the match—

MISS HARRIS
You felt the heat? . . .
(Maurie blinks once)

. . . It almost burned you? . . .
(Maurie blinks once)

. . . Now, try to blow the match out . . . before it burns you . . .

The match has burned low, and she lights another one and holds it a short distance from Maurie's mouth, and then moves it closer. Maurie stares intently at the match,—striving mightily to exhale voluntarily as it approaches his lips—

INT. ROYALS LOCKER ROOM—NIGHT

After the game, Jack is seated on the bench in front of his locker, a towel around his midsection, as he wearily drinks from a can. Seated beside him is a newspaperman. In the background, players are resting, dressing, etc.

REPORTER *(inquisitively, surprised)*
. . . But how did you do *that?*

JACK *(matter-of-factly)*

I went down to the courthouse . . . they gave me a bunch of papers . . .

he shrugs

REPORTER

But taking legal custody of someone is a complicated matter. What do you know about things like that? Didn't you have a lawyer?

JACK

Lawyers get fees. It wasn't so tough. I kept asking questions until I got answers.

REPORTER *(incredulous)*

And you made out the papers yourself?

JACK *(drily)*

This may come as a big shock to you, . . . but I can read and write.

Reporter shakes his head, impressed, as he makes some notes—

REPORTER

Damnedest thing I've ever heard.

JACK

Why? Somebody had to do it . . . sign papers . . . make decisions . . . pay bills . . .

REPORTER

What *are* you doing for money?

JACK *(shrugs)*

I'm still trying to figure that out . . .

(rises and stretches, painfully)

. . . God! I feel like I've been through a meat grinder . . .

REPORTER

Yeah . . . it was a tough game. How's Maurie coming along?

JACK   *(stretching and wincing)*

At the moment, I think he's in better shape than I am.

INT. PHYSICAL THERAPY ROOM—DAY

Maurie is stretched out on his stomach on one of the tables. One of the attendants is astraddle Maurie, his knee on the small of Maurie's back, his hands tightly grasping Maurie's shoulders, pulling his back up into an arched position. The second attendant supports Maurie's head with his hands. Rosie stands to one side, watching. Each time the arch of Maurie's back reaches an extreme angle, Maurie's expression projects the pain. The second attendant holding his head studies him closely to see if he seeks relief. But Maurie's eyes remain unblinking. Over this, Jack enters the Therapy Room. The first attendant disengages himself from the table and takes a deep breath—

FIRST ATTENDANT

I don't know about you, Maurie . . . but I could do with a break.

The attendants roll Maurie on to his back as Jack approaches the table.

JACK

Hi, Mo . . .

Maurie blinks once. As Rosie comes to him and bathes his perspiring face with a wet cloth—

JACK

You watch the game?
(Maurie blinks once)

. . . How'd you like it?

Maurice blinks twice and Jack looks at him, annoyed—

JACK

You're out of your mind! We beat them by 9 points. What's wrong with that?
(Maurie blinks several times)

. . . You're going to tell me what was wrong? . . .
(Maurie blinks once)

. . . Okay . . . first letter, first word . . . before 'M'? . . .
(Maurie blinks twice)

. . . after 'M'. N-O-P-Q-R-S-T-U- . . .
(Maurie blinks once)

. . . 'U'? Second letter . . .
(Maurie blinks twice)

. . . No? No second letter? . . .

(Maurie blinks once)

. . . *'You'* is the first word? . . .

(Maurie blinks once)

. . . Okay, first letter, second word . . . before 'M'? . . .

(Maurie blinks once)

. . . A-B-C-D-E-F-G-H-I-J-K-L . . .

(Maurie blinks once)

. . . First letter is *'L'* . . . second letter before 'M'? . . .

(Maurie blinks twice)

. . . After 'M' . . . M-N-O . . .

(Maurie blinks once)

. . . Second letter is *'O'* . . .*'L-O'* . . third letter before 'M'? . . .

(Maurie blinks twice)

. . . After 'M' . . . M-N-O-P-Q-R-S-T-U . . .

(Maurie blinks once)

. . . Third letter is *'U'* . . . *'L-O-U'* . . . Okay, fourth letter . . .

ROSIE   *(interrupts)*

You can stop right there. He's trying to tell you that you were lousy.

JACK

How do *you* know?

ROSIE

I watched the game, too.

Maurie chortles.

INT. ROYALS LOCKER ROOM—NIGHT

As Jack starts to change into his uniform, the trainer moves in carrying, with both hands, two thick
stacks of mail, which he places on Jack's bench—

TRAINER

Never knew you had so many fans . . .

JACK   (surprised, eying mail)

I don't.

He sits on the bench and opens one of the enve-
lopes. He reads a short note to which is attached a
check and stares at it, surprised. He opens another
envelope. Another note, another check. A third
envelope. No note, but a piece of currency. Dumbfounded, he opens another envelope and is staring
at another check as Richie moves into the shot—

RICHIE

Now, that's what I call fan mail!

JACK

I don't understand it. How come?

RICHIE

They read the newspapers. So do I . . .

(hands Jack a check)

. . . And I'm stingy.

Grinning, he moves away as Jack, still dazed, opens
another envelope.

INT. JACK'S DEN—TWYMAN HOME—NIGHT

He is seated at his desk, making some entries in a
ledger. Laid out on the desk are a pile of checks
and some currency,—also a pile of bills. Carole
enters, in dressing gown and quite pregnant—

CAROLE

You'd better get some sleep.

JACK

Just going over some of these bills. That column
is sure going to help pay a few of them . . .

He closes the ledger, turns off the desk lamp, rises
and moves to Carole. He puts his arm around her
waist and they move toward the interior foyer.

ANGLE IN FOYER

As they crossed foyer—

CAROLE

I forgot to tell you . . . Dorothy Parsons called
from New York today after you left. She's flying in
tomorrow afternoon . . . gets here at four.

Jack flips off the foyer light and they start up the
stairs—

JACK

I'll pick her up at the airport. She'll want to talk
to someone. And I guess I'm it.

Jack is preoccupied as they ascend the stairs.

MAIN ENTRANCE CORRIDOR
HOSPITAL—DAY

We pick up Jack and Dorothy as they come through
the main corridor.

> DOROTHY
> . . . Has he read my letters? . . .

> (Jack nods)
> . . . Any reaction?

> JACK   (shaking head)
> He can't react.

> DOROTHY   (somberly)
> Hasn't he made *any* progress?

> JACK
> Some. But it's so slight, you can hardly notice
> it . . .

EXT. COLUMNED WALK-WAY—TOWARD
MAIN HOSPITAL WING—DAY

> DOROTHY
> . . . Has he had any visitors?

> JACK   (shakes head)
> He hasn't wanted to see anyone . . . even the
> guys on the team.

> DOROTHY
> I hope he'll want to see me.

                            JACK

When he knows you're here? Of course
he will . . .

INT. ANGLE FROM RECEPTION AREA—
MAURIE'S WING

Jack and Dorothy enter Wing from outside walk-
way, move to reception area and stop—

                            JACK

I'd better prepare him . . .

Dorothy merely nods and stands there apprehen-
sively, as Jack moves away from reception area toward Maurie's room—

INT. MAURIE'S ROOM—DAY

He is in a semi-upright position in bed. Rosie is
feeding him by opening his mouth with her left
hand and inserting spoonsful of food deep into
his mouth, which he swallows. Jack enters and
moves to the bed—

                            JACK

Jeezuss! What a picnic you've got!

                            ROSIE

Hospital food's no picnic.

                            JACK

Then how come you got so round?

            ROSIE   *(wiping Maurie's mouth)*

I just serve it, I don't eat it . . .

MAURICE: If you were beautiful, that'd be great. Or if you were smart, that'd be very interesting. Or if you could cook up a storm, that'd be nice. But all three?

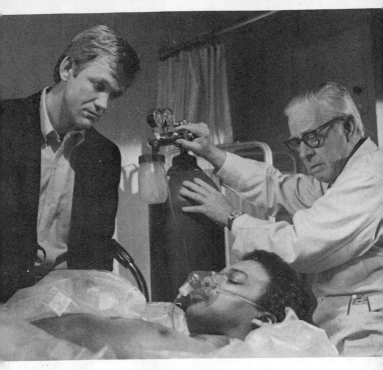

JACK: He'll make it, won't he?
DR. STEWART: He's a rugged fellow. That will help. . . .

DOCTOR: Good. That hurt, didn't it?

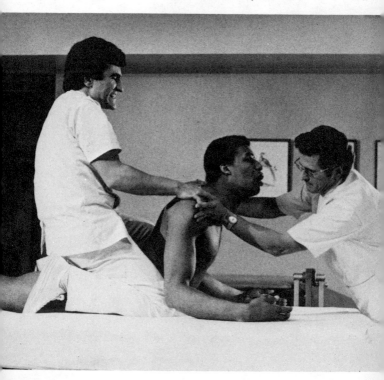

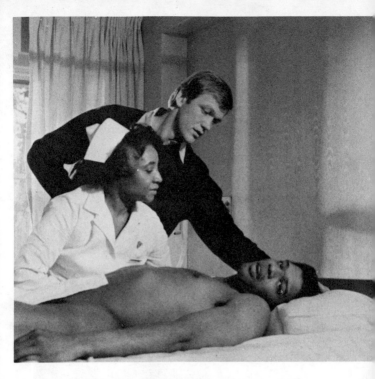

JACK: (*to Rosie*): How about coming over to the locker room after the game and giving *me* a massage? (*A muffled laugh from Maurice*)

ROSIE: What are you laughing at?
That'd be nice duty. All those big, handsome fellows in the locker room.

JACK: You're a dirty old woman.
ROSIE (*chuckling*): I'm not so old. . . .

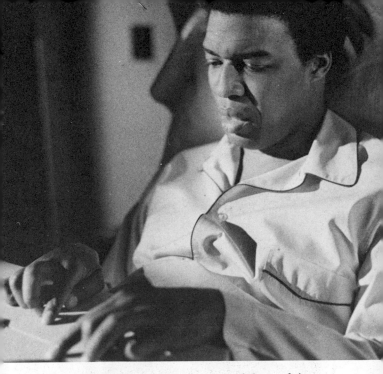

JACK (*broad impatience; he gestures elaborately*):
... You've been in here nine months! In nine months Carole came up with a baby boy! And *you* pick up a spoon? ...

JACK: Damn it, Mo, I can't send Dorothy away like that. Let me bring her in for a moment.
(*Maurice blinks twice*)

Okay ... if that's the way you want it. ...
As Jack leaves the room, Maurice lies unblinking—and gradually, his eyes fill with tears.

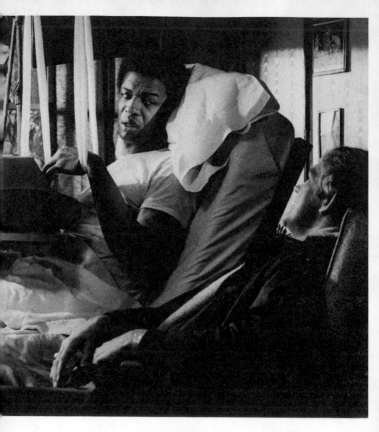

JACK: ... You want to say something?
Write a letter. ...

JACK: Okay, I've unloaded the tomato sauce.
Now I'd like to unload your girl.

JACK: Did you have a good time at the zoo, sweetie?
LISA: Oh, yes, Daddy . . . it was super!

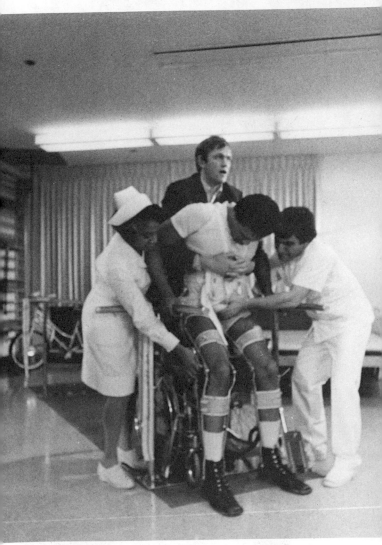

JACK: I thought all you fellows were supposed
to have rhythm. . . .

DOROTHY: Jack . . . thank you for letting me have this. Now, sell it. . . .

SID: This what you wanted?

DOROTHY: I hear we're going for a ride. . . .
MAURICE: We?

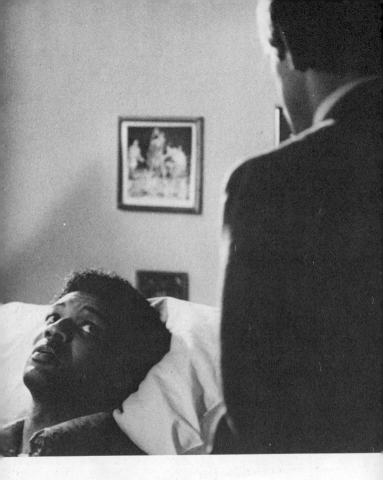

ANNOUNCER: ... say "hello" once again, to ...
Big Mo! ... Maurie Stokes! ...

MAURICE: Jack ... can I make a will?
JACK: I don't think so.
MAURICE: Why? Because you're my guardian?
JACK: Hell, that's got nothing to do with it.
To make a will, you have to be of sound mind.
And you're nuts!

JACK: Mo . . . thanks for helping make my night great.
MAURICE: Thanks for making my last 10 years great.

Chuckling, she gathers up the tray and exits the room.

JACK

She's a great gal . . .
(Maurie blinks once)

. . . and speaking of gals, I have a surprise for you . . .

Maurie stares at Jack and blinks his eyes several times.

JACK

Dorothy Parsons is outside.

For a long moment, Maurie stares at Jack—and then closes his eyes.

JACK (matter-of-factly)

She flew out from New York to see you.

Maurie opens his eyes, stares at Jack for just an instant, and then blinks his eyes twice.

JACK

Maybe you didn't understand . . . Dorothy is here to visit you. Okay?
(Maurie blinks twice)

. . . It's pretty damn nice of her to come all that way. I'll bring her in . . .
(Maurie blinks twice)

. . . You mean to tell me that she's standing right outside this door, and you refuse to see her? . . .

(Maurie blinks once)

. . . Damn it, Mo, I can't send her away like that.
Let me bring her in for a moment . . .

Maurie blinks twice. Jack studies him for just an
instant.

JACK   *(shrugging)*

Okay . . . if that's the way you want it . . .

As Jack moves to exit the room, the CAMERA
MOVES INTO A CLOSE HEAD SHOT—
MAURIE

He lies there, unblinking,—and, gradually, his
eyes fill with tears.

INT. HOSPITAL COMMISSARY—DAY

Jack and Dorothy are finishing lunch—

DOROTHY

. . . But I guess I can understand it. If it were
reversed, I'd probably feel the same way.

JACK

Sooner or later he'll reach a point where it won't
be so painful for him.

DOROTHY

You'll let me know, won't you? . . .

(Jack nods)

. . . Meantime, I'll just keep writing to him.

She sits there, sadly.

JACK *(a little smile)*

Cheer up.

DOROTHY

It's not easy.

JACK

You want some help? He's up in physical
therapy . . .

She looks at him, quizzically.

HOSPITAL CORRIDOR—EXT. PHYSICAL THERAPY ROOM

Jack and Dorothy move down the corridor toward
the doors to the Physical Therapy Room. As they
reach the doors, Jack stops and gestures with his
head toward one of the glass windows in the swing-
ing door—

JACK

Take a look . . .

Dorothy peers through the little window.

THEIR INTO PHYSICAL THERAPY ROOM

Maurie is stretched out on his stomach on one of
the tables. One therapist, his knees bent bracing
himself, has his hands under the front of Maurie's
shoulders, pushing them upward, so that his chest
is elevated from the table. Maurie's limp head is
supported by his chin resting against the attendant's chest. The second attendant has his left arm

firmly pinioned against the small of Maurie's back, with both of Maurie's legs cradled in his right arm with which he presses the legs up and back, rhythmically. Each time he thrusts Maurie's legs back, Maurie's expression reflects the pain he feels.

CLOSE SHOT—DOROTHY

At first, she reflects in anguish the pain she is witnessing. But, as she watches, her expression subtly changes—and gradually achieves a reflective satisfaction. If what she is witnessing has not exactly cheered her, it has reassured her.

Dorothy turns away from the window and looks at Jack. There is the faintest suggestion of a smile of confidence on her face—

> DOROTHY *(quietly)*
> You were right. I *do* feel better. He'll give it a hell of a fight . . .

EXT. MAIN HOSP. DRIVEWAY—NIGHT

Cab pulls up. Jack gets out, carrying suitcase, hands driver a bill and moves through main entrance. From the deserted condition of the surroundings we know it is very late at night—

INT. MAURIE'S ROOM—NIGHT

Maurie is lying in a semi-upright position. The bed table is extended over his torso. His arms lie on the table. Near the fingers of his right hand is a spoon. He is awake. Rosie is seated in a chair,

reading. Jack opens the door quietly and tiptoes in.
Rosie looks up—

ROSIE

No need to tiptoe around. He's not asleep.

JACK *(surprised)*

It's almost two o'clock.

ROSIE

I know. But he won't go to sleep.

JACK

Why not?

ROSIE

I think he's been waiting for you.

JACK

Plane just got in. What's wrong?

ROSIE *(a little smile)*

I think he wants to show you something . . .

Then she leaves the room. Jack approaches the bed
as Maurie's unblinking eyes look at him intently.

JACK

Do you? . . .
(Maurie blinks once)

. . . Okay. What?

Maurie's eyes turn from Jack to the spoon beside
his fingers. He concentrates mightily. The tempo
of his breathing gradually increases. His thumb

begins to quiver. And then his forefinger. Although the spoon is just an inch or two from his fingers it takes him perhaps ten or fifteen seconds to move his fingers, quivering, to where they are touching the curved, elevated part of the spoon. As he gets it between his thumb and forefinger, his eyes switch to Jack, for just an instant,—almost as if to say "now, watch this',—and then, his hand noticeably trembling, he tries to lift the end of the spoon. It takes him another ten or fifteen seconds, concentrating mightily. And then his fingers slowly rise about an inch from the table, the end of the spoon between them. He holds it for perhaps a couple of seconds. And then the spoon drops back to the table and his fingers relax limply upon it. His eyes turn quickly to stare at Jack,—who has been watching this intently but impassively. For just a beat, Jack stares at Maurie, and then his eyebrows go up—

JACK   *(broad impatience)*
You've *got* to be kidding! . . .

(glances at watch)
. . . It's two o'clock in the morning. I've played three games this week and just crawled off an airplane with my butt dragging. And you've got me standing here watching you *pick up a spoon?*

(he gestures elaborately)
. . . You've been in here nine months! In nine months, Carole came up with a baby boy! And *you* pick up a *spoon?* . . . that's not the most entertaining act I've ever seen . . .

(as he moves toward door)

I have to get some sleep. See you tomorrow . . .

As he exits—

CLOSE SHOT—MAURIE

He lies there, a slow smile spreading across his features.

INT. JACK'S DEN—TWYMAN HOME—
CLOSE SHOT JACK—AT DESK—DAY

He is on the telephone—

JACK *(with authority)*

. . . IBM? . . . I'd like to speak to somebody about a typewriter, an electric typewriter . . . no, not the Sales Department. I don't want to buy one . . . well, what I want is for IBM to *give* me one . . . you're right, Miss, it *is* a little unusual . . . who's the President of your company?

INT. MAURIE'S ROOM—DAY

Maurie is propped up in a semi-sitting position. A tubular frame has been placed over the bed. From it hang two long slings. Rosie is on one side of the bed, Jack on the other. They are placing Maurie's wrists into the two slings. On the bed-table is an electric typewriter. Maurie's hands are suspended several inches above the keyboard. Rosie and Jack adjust flaps on the two slings, lowering Maurie's limp hands, until his fingers are touching the keys of the typewriter. As they are doing this—

JACK

. . . I'm getting a little tired of you blinking your eyes at me all the time. You want to say something? Write a letter. There . . . that ought to do it.

Maurie's eyes look up at Jack, and then at the type-writer.

FULL ESTABLISHING SHOT—NEW YORK ARENA—NIGHT

The traffic, crowds, marquee, etc.

INT. PRESS LOUNGE—NIGHT

Members of the press are having drinks and sand-wiches after the game. Jack is in one corner of the lounge, being interviewed by several newspaper men. MILTON KUTSHER comes through the door. He looks around, sees Jack and moves into the room, waiting for Jack to be free of his infor-mal interview. After a moment—

ANOTHER ANGLE ON JACK AND NEWS-PAPER MEN

JACK

. . . but do me a favor, fellows, will ya? If you write anything, tell what a battle Mo is putting up.

FIRST NEWSPAPER MAN

Seems to me you're putting up quite a fight, too.

JACK   *(shaking head)*

Nothing compared to what he's doing. Make sure you write *that*.

SECOND NEWSPAPER MAN

You let us know if there's anything else we can to
to help.

JACK   *(smiles)*

You can count on it . . .

He picks up his duffelbag and moves away from
group toward door.

ANOTHER ANGLE

As Jack moves toward the door, Milton Kutsher approaches, extending his hand.

KUTSHER

Mr. Twyman . . . I'm Milton Kutsher.

JACK   *(pausing)*

Hi . . .

KUTSHER   *(very soft-spoken)*

Could we have a little talk?

JACK   *(politely)*

Well, Mr. . . .

(hesitates)

KUTSHER

Kutsher . . . Milton Kutsher.

JACK

Well, Mr. Kutsher . . . I have to hit the sack . . .
early plane in the morning.

KUTSHER   *(quietly firm)*

I understand. But I think we should talk. I heard

that you've been having trouble trying to set up a benefit game for Stokes.

JACK *(nods)*

Every player in the league has volunteered to appear. The problem is to get an arena.

KUTSHER

Plenty of those around.

JACK

But the overhead eats you up. By the time you get done paying for the arena, the staff, insurance, promotion, programs . . . all the expenses of staging a thing like this . . . there wouldn't be much left.

KUTSHER

How much were you hoping to clear on the game?

JACK

10 . . . maybe 15 thousand. But there's no way, with the overhead.

KUTSHER

Then 3,000 seats at $5.00 a seat would do it?

JACK

But that's gross, not net.

KUTSHER *(simply)*

That would be net.

Jack studies him for just a beat, then moves to one of the settees and they sit.

JACK *(perplexed)*

Do you own an arena?

KUTSHER   *(shaking head)*

No. I've got a hotel in upstate New York . . . in Monticello.

JACK   *(still puzzled)*

But how could we play a game like that in a hotel?

KUTSHER   *(matter-of-factly)*

Leave that to me. Let me ask you something else. Even if you clear 15,000, don't you still have a lot, more money to raise?

JACK   *(nodding)*

We get a couple of thousand a month from Workmen's Compensation . . .

KUTSHER

Does that cover everything?

JACK

Hell, no. I still have to raise another 5 or 6 thousand every month.

KUTSHER

How?

JACK

Oh, fund-raising drives with various organizations . . . that sort of thing. But mostly, the press. They've been great. All over the country. There was a column in one of the papers here in New York, and over $3,000 came in. After a column in Boston, I received a letter from a family who said that they spend $500 on their Christmas every year, and they enclosed a check for $500.

KUTSHER
Nice.

JACK

Sports Illustrated . . . the papers in Los Angeles
. . . Chicago . . . Philadelphia . . . all over the
country . . . to meet my budget each month, I
contact one of them, they run a column, and people respond.

KUTSHER *(smiling)*
Maybe there's some hope for the human race. I
guess this game would have to be played after the
season's over? . . .

(Jack nods)
. . . Okay, that gives us a few months . . .

He takes a card from his pocket and hands it to
Jack.

KUTSCHER
You write and tell me exactly what you'll need.
I'll take it from there.

JACK *(staring hard)*
Why? Why would you do that?

KUTSCHER *(gently, a little smile)*
You're a hell of a one to be asking *that* question . . .

INT. HOSPITAL CORRIDOR—NEAR
MAURIE'S ROOM—DAY

Rosie comes out of the room carrying a large

bundle of soiled linens. As she deposits them in
the laundry chute, near the door to Maurie's room,
Jack moves into the shot toward Maurie's door—

ROSIE

Welcome back . . .

JACK

How's it going, Rosie?

ROSIE

Only one complaint . . . he's wearing me out.

JACK   *(smiling)*

You're tougher than that.

ROSIE

Never ran into anyone like him. He wants to be
doing something every minute. He gets finished
with therapy, you think he'll just lie there in bed
and rest? . . .

(shakes head)

. . . He just keeps working at *something*. He's
been at that typewriter ever since you left . . .
morning, noon and night . . .

JACK

That's good for him. What's he writing?

ROSIE

A letter.

JACK

Who to?

ROSIE

You. You'd better take a look at it. It took him
a week to write it.

Jack enters Maurie's room—

INT. MAURIE'S ROOM

The bed-table, with the typewriter on it, is beside the bare bed. Still inserted in the typewriter
is a sheet of paper, Jack pulls the paper from the
roll and looks at it. Almost immediately, it is
obvious that what he sees has hit him in the gut—

VERY CLOSE INSERT—THE LETTER

The words are badly spaced, some of them run
together,—and some of the letters have been "x'd"
out. It is as badly typed as possible. And the disarray of letters and words betrays the long and
painful effort that went into it. But it's legible,
and it reads—

Dear Jack—How will I ever be able to thank
you?—Mo

INT. PHYSICAL THERAPY ROOM—DAY

Maurie is in one of the therapy tanks,—only his
head above water, supported by a cushion of thick,
rolled-up towels. One of the male therapists is in
the tank with Maurie, manipulating various parts
of his body,—as Jack enters, the letter in his hand.
He moves to the side of the tank. The therapist
gets out of the tank. As he dries himself off—

THERAPIST
Okay, Mo . . . you can relax a while.

As he exits, Jack moves closer to Maurie, holding the letter. Maurie stares at him.

JACK
Rosie says it took you a week to type this. Right now, I don't know how you can thank me. But, believe me, I'll think of something. 'Cause if you think I'm going through all this for nothing, you're out of your—you should excuse the expression—cotton-pickin' mind. And when I figure out some way you can thank me, you'll be the first to know. Okay?

A little smile appears on Maurice's face, as he looks up at Jack. And then, slowly, his lips form an open circle. And after a second or two, a muffled, strained sound comes from them—

MAURIE *(very slowly)*
O . . . kay . . .

As Jack stares down at Maurie, articulating his first word, the therapist re-enters the room.

JACK *(to therapist)*
Now, we've really got trouble. Once he starts talking, we'll never be able to shut him up . . .

INT. TWYMAN HOME—LIVING ROOM— DAY

Jack is on the telephone—

JACK *(dumbfounded)*

You've got *what*? . . . a *thousand cases*? . . . you
sure they're for me? . . . but what am I going to
do with them? . . . okay . . . I'll be down . . .
thanks . . .

As he talks, Carole enters the living room. He hangs
up—

JACK

Now that's the damnedest thing I've ever heard!
Some cannery has sent a contribution for Maurie
. . . are you ready? . . . a *thousand cases of
tomato sauce!*

CAROLE *(grinning)*

Well, that could come in handy . . . if we all live
forever . . .

JACK

It's piled up at a warehouse down at the railroad
yard. And if I don't get it out of there, I'll have to
pay storage.

CAROLE *(amused)*

What are you going to do?

JACK *(distraught)*

What I'm *not* going to do is pay storage. I've got
to find a grocery chain . . . or something like that
. . . and sell the stuff off . . .

He rises and starts from the room.

CAROLE

You promised to take Lisa to the Zoo this afternoon.

JACK *(hurriedly)*

I know. I'm sorry, honey. But I've got to unload this stuff . . .

(broadly sardonic)

. . . All of a sudden I'm peddling tomato sauce! . . .

As he hurriedly exits the room, Carole stands there,—somewhat troubled.

CLOSE ANGLE—MONKEY HOUSE AT ZOO —DAY

Brief footage of some monkeys at their typical, funny play. CAMERA PULLS BACK TO RE-VEAL CAROLE & LISA WATCHING. Lisa is now about 5 years old.

CLOSE ANGLE—CAROLE & LISA

Carole is giggling at the antics of the monkeys. She glances down at Lisa who watches the monkeys, strangely soberly.

CAROLE *(lightly)*

Aren't they funny?

LISA *(not with it)*

I guess so.

CAROLE

I thought you'd love the monkeys.

LISA

I wish Daddy were here.

CAROLE

I bet he wishes he were, too.

LISA

If he did, he'd be here.

CAROLE *(placatingly)*

He really couldn't help it, dear. He had to do something for his friend today.

LISA *(frowning)*

I don't like his friend.

For just a beat, Carole digests this thoughtfully.

CAROLE *(softly)*

There's something else I think you should see, dear.

LISA *(disinterestedly)*

Some more animals?

CAROLE

No.

She takes Lisa's hand and they move away from the monkey cage.

INT. THERAPY ROOM—DAY

Maurie, his legs, torso and neck in heavy braces, is upright between two parallel bars, his hands resting on the bars. And once again, we are dramatically reminded of his massive stature. Rosie stands on one side of him and a therapist on the other,—both dwarfed by his enormity. As he stands there, partly supporting himself,—but mostly supported by Rosie and the therapist,—he is laughing. Rosie and the therapist are smiling broadly. Off to one side, Jack gestures with broad irritability—

JACK

. . . It was like having a hot ferry boat on your hands. A thousand cases of tomato sauce! All I needed was 4 tons of spaghetti!

Maurie's laugh becomes uproarious,—and he almost topples over. As Rosie and the therapist support him—

ROSIE *(laughing)*
What did you do with it?

JACK *(a broad shrug)*
I peddled it. And I'm a pretty damn good peddler. Got $4,700 from Kroeger's.

ROSIE
You had me worried for a while. I thought that maybe next week I'd be paid off in tomato sauce.

THERAPIST *(smiling)*
I hate to intrude on all this big business . . .

(to Maurie)
. . . But you've got about a foot to go.

MAURIE *(slowly, strained)*
O . . . kay . . .

Jack watches as—with great effort—Maurie, aided

by the therapist, moves his right hand a couple of inches, followed by a couple of inches with his right foot. Then, his left hand, and his left foot. Tortuously, he forces his massive body to move the remaining 12 inches on the bars. Then, quickly, the therapist rolls a wheel chair behind him and Rosie and the therapist ease Maurie in to it. His face is covered with sweat. As Rosie wipes his face—

THERAPIST

How do you feel, Mo?

MAURIE

Great . . .

ANOTHER ANGLE

Jack moves beside them, as Rosie pushes the wheel chair out of the Therapy Room.

ANGLE IN CORRIDOR—MOVING SHOT

As they move down the corridor—

JACK

You really feel great?

Maurie certainly doesn't look great, seated in the wheel chair, his entire body braced, and his face reflecting the strain and exhaustion of his efforts at therapy.

MAURIE

Sure . . .

JACK

Okay. I've unloaded the tomato sauce. Now I'd like to unload your girl.

Maurie makes a slight movement with his neck and stares up at Jack.

JACK

And don't give me any fish-eyes. She's been writing to you regularly. And I've been talking to her on the phone. What the hell more can I say to her? She wants to see you.

MAURIE

No . . .

JACK

Look, Mo . . . I'm not *asking* you. I'm *telling* you. She's a great girl. And what in hell she was doing with you I'll *never* know. But she's been pretty damn patient. And I'm running out of excuses why she can't see you.

They have reached Maurie's room and Rosie wheels him in, Jack following.

ANOTHER ANGLE—IN CORRIDOR—TO-WARD RECEPTION AREA

The elevator door opens and Carole and Lisa, hand in hand, Carole and Lisa moved into shot. As Lisa looks around, wonderingly, Carole leads her across the Reception Area toward the door to Maurie's room, which is open.

CLOSER ANGLE—AT MAURIE'S DOOR—OVER CAROLE & LISA—INTO ROOM

Inside the room, Rosie and Jack are wheeling
Maurie's chair up to the side of the bed. Jack,
Rosie, and Maurie are unaware of Carole and
Lisa standing in the corridor, looking into the
room.

ROSIE

I'll get the orderlies.

JACK

Oh, come on, we can do it . . .

ROSIE   *(archly)*

Be my guest . . .

As Jack takes his jacket off, Rosie removes the blanket which covers Maurie, seated in the wheel chair,
and reveals the heavy braces covering his legs, torso and neck. Jack bends over, gets one arm under
Maurie's shoulders and the other under Maurie's
behind. As Rosie wraps her arms around Maurie's
legs—

CLOSE SHOT—CAROLE & LISA

Holding her mother's hand, Lisa watches, trans-
fixed. Her eyes almost pop from the impact of what
she is witnessing. She may not fully comprehend
what is going on. But, for the first time, she becomes aware of the enormity of her father's in-
volvement with 'his friend'.

INT. ROOM

Jack and Rosie set their legs sturdily—

ROSIE

One . . . two . . . three . . .

On 'three', Jack lifts Maurie from the chair, as
Rosie kicks it clear. As Jack gets Maurie clear of the
chair, we can see that it is an enormous burden.
Jack's eyes pop—

JACK *(gasping)*

God!

With a great effort, they manage to move him the
short distance from the chair to the bed. As they
plop him on to it, both exhale in relief.

ROSIE *(to Maurie, mock complaint)*
Why couldn't you have been a jockey?

JACK *(straightening up)*
Well, I can't think of a better place to get a hernia.

As Rosie and Jack start to unstrap Maurie's braces,
twisting and turning his body and flexing his legs
to do so—

CLOSE SHOT—CAROL & LISA

As they watch, Lisa totally immersed in what she
sees, Carole lets go of Lisa's hand, puts her arms
around Lisa's shoulder and hugs her closely.

INT. MAURIE'S ROOM

Rosie and Jack are just getting the last brace off
Maurie—

JACK   *(to Maurie)*

So I'm going to tell her she can come next Friday,
after she finishes work in New York.

MAURIE

No . . .

JACK

Damn it, *yes!* What the hell are you afraid of?
That you don't look so good? Let me tell you
something . . . you were *never* any beauty! She'll
be here Friday . . .

ANGLE IN CORRIDOR—OUTSIDE
MAURIE'S ROOM

Carole and Lisa, without a word, move slowly
away from Maurie's door toward the Reception
Area.

INT. MAURIE'S ROOM

Putting on his jacket, Jack exits the room, mum-
bling to himself. As Rosie covers Maurie with a
sheet—

MAURIE

Tape . . .

Rosie slides the bed-table over Maurie, picks up a
small tape machine from a side table and places
it on the bed-table. (The following procedure is
done quickly and deftly. Obviously, it has been
done many times before.) She lowers one of the
overhead slings, places Maurie's right wrist in it,

so that his hand is right in front of his mouth.

RECEPTION AREA

Carole and Lisa, hand in hand, stand in the Reception Area, facing toward Maurie's room. As Jack approaches from the room, he stops, astonished at seeing them there. There is just a beat and then, deeply moved, Lisa breaks away from Carole, runs to him and jumps into his arms, her arms tightly around his neck. Carrying her, as she hugs him, Jack moves toward Carole. For just a beat, Carole and Jack look at each other, silently communicating.

JACK   *(to Lisa)*

Did you have a good time at the Zoo, sweetie?

LISA

Oh, yes, Daddy . . . it was super!

As she kisses him on the cheek, and they turn and move off.

INT. MAURIE'S ROOM

Rosie is applying some tape, sticking the microphone of the recorder to the fingers of Maurie's right hand which, in the sling, is in front of his mouth. Then she places his left hand on the tape machine, carefully positioning his fingers.

ROSIE

Okay . . . now, sing MELANCHOLY BABY . .

And she leaves the room.

(*Maurie's speech is slow, strained and guttural. And some words are more articulate than others. But the gist of what he is saying comes across.*)

Maurie pushes one of the buttons on the machine with a finger of his left hand.

> Maurie *(into microphone)*
> Hel—lo . . . How . . . are . . . you . . . I . . . am fine . . . Thank . . . you . . . for . . . your . . . letters . . . . What . . . have . . . you . . . been . . . doing. . . . You're . . . lucky . . . I . . . won't . . . ask . . . you . . . to . . . dance . . .

A sad, nostalgic smile touches his face. Hs pushes another button on the machine, stopping it. Then he pushes another button,—and listens intently as the recorded words play back to him. He pushes a button, stopping the machine. And then another button, restarting it.

> Maurie
> Hel . . . lo . . . . . How . . . are . . . you . . . . . I am fine . . .

INT. HOSPITAL—MAURIE'S CORRIDOR—NIGHT

Jack and Dorothy stand in corridor a few feet from door to Maurie's room. Dorothy is obviously deeply engulfed in the emotion of the moment. Jack studies her compassionately. After a moment, Rosie comes out of Maurie's room. As she approaches Jack and Dorothy, we can see that she, too, is sub-

ject to some strain and tension. She merely nods
and goes off up the corridor.

JACK   *(to Dorothy)*
Okay?

Dorothy directs a thin smile of reassurance at Jack,
and moves slowly toward Maurie's door, head
lowered. She hesitates for just a beat at the door,—
then straightens up and enters Maurie's room—

INT. MAURIE'S ROOM

He is in the wheel chair beside the bed. Rosie has
covered him up to his neck with a coverlet, hiding
the braces which keep him upright. The door
opens and Dorothy bounces in spiritedly—

DOROTHY   *(persuasively brightly)*
I hate the phrase myself . . . but long time no
see . . .

Dorothy moves to the bed and sits on the side of
it, smiling brightly.

MAURIE
Hello . . .

DOROTHY
Hi . . .

MAURIE
I . . . am . . . fine . . .

DOROTHY
I can see that.

MAURIE

How . . . are . . . you?

DOROTHY

I'm great . . .

(grins)

. . . as long as you don't ask me to dance.

MAURIE *(smiling)*

I . . . am . . . glad . . . to . . . see . . . you . . .

EXT. CINCINNATI AIRPORT—PASSAGE-
WAY TO GATES—NIGHT

CAMERA MOVES with Jack and Dorothy as they
walk slowly along the area—

JACK

. . . You were great with him.

DOROTHY

That wasn't difficult.

JACK *(nodding)*

I know what you mean. It's the damnedest thing.
When stuff piles up on me . . . I'm teed off
at the coach . . . or we blow an important game
. . . or the bills are coming in faster than the
money . . . when I've *had* it. I spend time with
him, and I feel *great*. Everybody feels the same way
about him. He's the best therapy in that hospital.

DOROTHY

I'm not surprised.

JACK

He's been through hell. And there hasn't been a moment when he hasn't been cheerful . . . hopeful . . .

CLOSE ANGLE—DEPARTURE GATE

They stop. As people board in the background, Dorothy looks up at Jack—

DOROTHY *(quietly)*

Don't you believe it.

JACK *(earnestly)*

Take my word for it. Nobody has seen him falter for a second.

DOROTHY

Nobody has *seen* him falter. He'd never allow that. But he has. Alone . . . at night . . . there've been those moments when he's wondered . . . and he's doubted. And he's cried.

JACK

Big Mo? *Cry?*

DOROTHY *(simply)*

I could never love a man who wouldn't.

She reaches up, kisses his cheek, turns and moves toward the airplane.

INT. PHYSICAL THERAPY ROOM—DAY

Naked, except for a pair of brief shorts, Maurie stands in the middle of the room,—as always, his entire body in braces and his arms hanging limply at his sides. In front of him, about arm's length, hangs a contraption which looks like a trapeze bar. One attendant stands beside Maurie, supporting him upright,—as a second attendant, working a pulley, lowers the bar to the level of Maurie's shoulders. Dr. Walker stands off to one side, observing. One at a time, the second attendant lifts Maurie's arms and curls Maurie's fingers around the bar. There is a leather attachment on the bar which he affixes to each of Maurie's wrists. The first attendant steps away from Maurie, as the second attendant, working the pulley, slowly raises the level of the trapeze bar. As they are doing this, Jack enters the room, moves to Dr. Walker, and also watches. The bar is elevated until Maurie's arms are fully extended above his head. The second attendant strains on the pulley, so that Maurie's body is really hanging from his arms, his feet only lightly touching the floor. As this occurs, Maurie's expression reflects the strain and pain.

DR. WALKER *(quietly)*
All right, Maurie . . . try to take a few steps . . .

With enormous effort, Maurie tries to move his legs,—which, barely touching the floor, are not supporting the full weight of his body. He manages a few awkward, ill-directed short steps.

JACK *(drily)*
I thought all you fellows were supposed to have rhythm . . .

Even in his painful effort, Maurie chuckles. After
a few moments of this awkward, almost macabre
dance, the second attendant lowers the bar and
unfastens Maurie's hands from it, as the first attendant slides the wheel chair behind Maurie and
lowers him into it. Maurie is panting from his
effort.

> DR. WALKER *(to attendants)*
> Let's get the tank ready . . .

As he and attendants move out of the shot—

> JACK
> I heard from Milt Kutsher this morning. He said
> he'll be ready to stage the game three weeks from
> Saturday.

(At this point, Maurie's speech is noticeably more
articulate than heretofore. But it is still slower than
normal and with obvious conscious effort.)

> MAURIE
> You going to play?

> JACK
> Sure . . .
>
> *(grandly)*
> . . . I'll probably be high scorer . . .

> MAURIE
> Fat chance . . .

The two attendants move back into the shot. They
are carrying a canvas hammock-like contraption,

which is suspended horizontally from an overhead
trolley. They place it beside Maurie's wheel chair.
And then, Jack assisting, they lift Maurie from the
wheel chair and lie him on his back on the ham-
mock. They remove his braces and guide the ham-
mock over to and above the tank and lower
Maurie into the tank, until only his head is above
water, supported by a cushion of towels. As the
attendants exit the shot, Jack sits on the side of
the tank, silent for a moment.

JACK

Mo . . . there's something I've been wanting to
ask you. And I've waited till you could talk a little.
The night they took you to the hospital they gave
me your personal effects to hold . . .

He reaches into his pocket and takes out the small
velvet ring-box—

JACK

I've been holding onto this. What do you want me
to do with it?

Maurie stares hard at the box, and his eyes darken.
But he doesn't say anything. Jack opens the box
and shows the ring to Maurie.

JACK

It *is* yours, isn't it?

For a long moment, Maurie stares at the ring, and
it appears as if he might crack. But he controls
himself.

JACK *(matter-of-factly)*
What do you want me to do with it?

MAURIE *(after a beat, softly)*
Sell it.

JACK
You must have bought it for something . . . for
someone. Tell me what to do.

MAURIE *(stronger)*
Sell it.

JACK
Now, look . . . you didn't buy the thing to sell
it. You must have had something in mind.

MAURIE
It's worth $2,000. Sell it and pay some bills.

JACK *(impatiently)*
Come on, Mo, I'm not prying! . . . I just want
to know . . .

MAURIE *(interrupts, very firmly)*
Don't argue with me.

Jack throws up his hands and rises from the side
of the tank—

JACK
Okay, rockhead . . . see you later . . .

(casually, as he moves off)
. . . Dorothy'll be here tomorrow night . . .

As Jack exits the Therapy Room—

CLOSE SHOT—MAURIE

His eyes betray the intense emotion he is feeling. He squeezes them shut,—vainly trying to erase his torment.

DESK AND RECEPTION AREA—MAURIE'S FLOOR

Rosie is standing at the desk, having some coffee with the Floor Nurse, as Jack enters shot. As he moves toward Rosie we hear, from the direction of Maurie's room, loud laughter (Dorothy's and Maurie's).

JACK

What's going on in there?

ROSIE *(wryly)*

I'm afraid to find out.

INT. MAURIE'S ROOM—NIGHT

Maurie is propped up in bed,—Dorothy is seated on the edge of the bed, smiling—

MAURIE

. . . So Billy got up . . . to go to the bathroom . . . not a stitch on . . . half asleep . . . opened the door . . . it locked behind him . . . and he was out in the hall . . .

DOROTHY *(laughing heartily)*

Then what happened?

MAURIE

He knocked . . . but I was asleep . . . never

heard him . . . and the house dick grabbed him.

They both are laughing uproariously as Jack and
Rosie enter—

                    ROSIE *(mock-scolding)*
You two are keeping the whole floor awake.

                    DOROTHY *(contritely)*
I'm sorry, Rosie. We'll simmer down . . .

                    ROSIE
Not now you won't. He has to sleep.

As Dorothy rises—

                    MAURIE
I'm not sleepy.

                    ROSIE
Then you'll just lie there. But the party's over for
tonight.

                    JACK
I'll drive you back, Dorothy . . .

Dorothy bends down and kisses Maurie's cheek.

                    DOROTHY
                    (straightens up, grins)
. . . and don't worry . . . if I have to go to the
bathroom tonight, I'll wear something . . .

As Maurie laughs—Jack and Dorothy exit the
room.

EXT. MOTEL—NIGHT

Jack's car pulls up and stops. He gets out, goes around, and opens the door for Dorothy.

DOROTHY (getting out)

Thanks for the lift, Jack. See you tomorrow . . .

JACK

Dorothy . . . there was something in Maurie's pocket the night they took him to the hospital. I've been holding it. He doesn't know I'm doing this . . . but I have a feeling it was meant for you . . . and that you should have it . . .

He takes the ring-box from his pocket and hands it to Dorothy—

JACK

. . . See you tomorrow . . .

And without further word, Jack gets into the car and drives off.

CLOSE SHOT—DOROTHY

She opens the box, and stares at the ring. And it tears at her insides.

INT. DOROTHY'S MOTEL ROOM—NIGHT

She comes out of the bathroom, in nightgown,—still deeply shaken. She moves slowly to the bed and gets in.

She reaches up and turns out the light. And then she lies there on her back,—eyes open and tortured. After a long moment—

LARGER ANGLE

She gets out of bed and moves to the bureau. She picks up the box, takes out the ring, and slips it on to her left ring finger. And then she moves back to the bed and gets in—

CLOSE ANGLE—DOROTHY

Slowly, she rolls over on to her side and clasps her hands beneath her face, the ring close to her cheek. And as her eyes brim with tears—

INT. RECEPTION AREA—MAURIE'S FLOOR—DAY

Jack and Dr. Walker are leaning against the floor desk.

DR. WALKER

. . . And while we will continue his general over-all therapy, I think it's time we got started on some occupational therapy.

JACK *(nodding)*

Sounds good.

DR. WALKER

Can you handle it?

JACK

One of the papers in St. Louis is doing a column next week. That should be good for a couple of thousand. And with the proceeds from the game . . . you go ahead and do whatever has to be done. I'll keep up with you, somehow.

DR. WALKER   *(a little smile)*
I bet you will . . .

As he moves away, Dorothy approaches from the elevator. Jack nods toward Maurie's room—

JACK
They're going to let him go out on the terrace today.

DOROTHY
That'll be nice . . .

JACK   *(glancing at watch)*
I have a fund raising luncheon . . . see you next week?

Dorothy nods,—and then takes the ring-box from her purse—

DOROTHY
Jack, thank you for letting me have this. Now, sell it . . .

She hands the box to Jack. He looks at her for a moment—

JACK
You sure?

She nods and manages a small, reassuring smile. Then, as if tearing herself away from an important part of her life, she turns and moves slowly toward Maurie's room—fighting the sadness within her. For an instant, she pauses at the door,—and then enters.

INT. MAURIE'S ROOM

He is in his wheel chair, beside the bed. Rosie is tucking blankets around him. Dorothy strides in briskly and radiantly—

> DOROTHY
>
> I hear we're going for a ride . . .

> MAURIE
>
> We?

> DOROTHY *(brightly)*
>
> I'm the driver.

> MAURIE
>
> That's all I need . . . a woman driver.

> DOROTHY
>
> Don't knock it 'til you've tried it.

> ROSIE
>
> You two going to talk about it, or do it?

> MAURIE *(to Rosie)*
>
> Don't wait up for us . . .

> ROSIE
>
> How far do you think you're going?

> MAURIE *(to Dorothy)*
>
> How about the West Wing?

> DOROTHY
>
> The West Wing it is . . .

> MAURIE
>
> If I'm lucky . . . she'll run out of gas . . . and park somewhere.

ROSIE   *(to Dorothy)*

If he has to fight for his honor, you've got it made.

FULL PANORAMIC SHOT—ROLLING
COUNTRYSIDE—DAY

A golf cart moves along the country road. Milton
Kutsher is driving, Carole beside him, Jack perched
on the rear deck.

ANOTHER ANGLE

The golf cart turns off the country road and
through the entrance gate, which identifies the
place as "Kutsher's Hotel and Country Club".
The cart moves along the main entrance driveway,
bordering the golf course. We see golfers on the
course, others going by in golf carts. Along the
other side of the road several guests go by on horse-
back.

CLOSER ANGLE—NEAR MAIN BUILDING
AND TERRACE

The golf cart swings past the swimming pool and
stops just below the terrace,—on which various
guests are lunching and drinking. Jack, Carole, and
Kutsher get off the cart and move onto the terrace.

CLOSER ANGLE—ON TERRACE

Jack and Carole look around, obviously impressed—

                    JACK   *(amazed)*
. . . Milton, I had no idea it was this kind of a
place.

                KUTSHER   *(shrugs, a little smile)*
It just grew.

                CAROLE   *(pop-eyed)*
What did you start with?

                KUTSHER   *(self-effacingly)*
Oh . . . a few acres . . . we could handle about
50 people.

                    JACK
And now?

                KUTSHER   *(simply)*
About a thousand. Let's take a look at the basketball court . . .

                JACK   *(a little smile)*
I've been *waiting* for that . . .

MOVING SHOT—JACK, CAROLE &
KUTSHER

                    JACK
If you've got a thousand people, how are you going
to draw 3,000?

                KUTSHER   *(assuredly)*
They'll be over from some of the other hotels . . .
and a lot of people are driving up from New
York . . .

JACK

Milt . . . all this work you've done . . . and putting thirty guys up for a couple of days . . . what's it costing?

KUTSHER (*shrugging it off*)
I haven't kept track. . . .

MED. SHOT—PATH BEHIND MAIN BLDG. —NEAR TENTH TEE—NIGHT

Jack and Carole move slowly along the path,— the hotel visible in one direction,—the rolling back nine and the surrounding hills visible in the other direction.

CLOSE TWO SHOT—MOVING

After a moment, as they walk—

CAROLE (*almost to herself*)
I'm glad we didn't bring the kids . . .

(*she looks up at Jack*)
. . . Does that sound awful?

He puts his arm around her and pulls her close to him.

JACK
I know what you mean.

They walk silently for a few moments, and then Jack notices a bench near the tenth tee and leads Carole toward it.

CLOSE ANGLE—AT BENCH

As they sit, he puts his arm around her shoulder, drawing her close to him. And they sit silently for a moment—

> JACK *(gently)*
> How rough has it been?

> CAROLE *(looking up at him)*
> Straight?

> JACK
> Straight.

> CAROLE *(wryly)*
> Sometimes . . . I think I've wished it was another woman.

> JACK *(dismally)*
> God! . . .

She looks up at him and shakes her head, reprovingly.

> CAROLE *(emphatically)*
> You are a dummy.

> JACK
> No argument . . .

> *(a beat)*
> Honey, why didn't you squawk?

> CAROLE *(straightforwardly)*
> I was too selfish to squawk.

JACK *(perplexed)*

You've lost me.

CAROLE *(candidly)*

There were times, especially at the start, when it was rough not having you around much. But gradually, I realized how much everybody was doing. Maurie, fighting every hour of every day. His parents, mortgaging their lives. Dorothy. And you. And I finally realized that the best way . . . the only way . . . that I could help . . . that I could do something . . . was to keep my big mouth shut . . .

Jack leans close and kisses her tenderly.

JACK *(softly)*

We have a lot to be grateful for, don't we?

CAROLE

I've known that for a long time . . .

Smiling, Jack rises and pulls her up into his arms and kisses her lightly

JACK

Okay . . . let's celebrate that.

CAROLE

Fine with me.

JACK

Milt's staging a big show tonight.

CAROLE *(deadpan)*

No show.

JACK *(deadpan)*
Just what did you have in mind?

CAROLE
You really *are* a dummy! . . .

INT. MAURIE'S ROOM

He is in his wheel chair, watching the television set. Dorothy is seated beside him. The action of the game is being shown. Maurie watches intently, eyes glowing—

MAURIE
Man! They're really goin' at it . . .

(a moment)
. . . Hey! . . . Oscar faked Jack right out of his shoes! . . .

Dorothy studies Maurie, poignantly relishing his enjoyment of the game. Rosie enters the room, puts something on the side table, and glances at the TV set for just a moment. Then she turns to leave—

DOROTHY
Aren't you going to watch, Rosie?

ROSIE *(shrugging)*
Not much interested, if Big Mo isn't playing.

MAURIE
If I could play, there'd be no game . . .

As Dorothy smiles, HOLD ON GAME ACTION

ON TELEVISION SET BRIEFLY and then—
INT. OCCUPATIONAL THERAPY ROOM—
DAY

Various patients are engaged in a variety of occupational therapy,—pottery kilns, woodwork,
etc. Maurie, in his wheel chair, is at one side of
the room, beside a young girl who is at a pottery wheel, shaping a small bowl. There is a board
resting on the arms of Maurie's chair. On it is
another small, unfinished bowl. Beside it are two
small paint cups. Maurie's right hand rests on the
board,—and a paint brush is taped to his fingers. He
is staring critically at the bowl the young woman
is working on—

MAURIE
That looks fine . . .

(Except for a slightly slower tempo, and a barely
perceptible effort with his tongue and lips,
Maurie's speech is almost normal.)

As the young woman resumes shaping of the bowl,
Maurie addresses himself to the bowl on the board
over his lap. Very slowly, patiently concentrating,
Maurie lifts his hand, dips the brush into a paint
cup and then slowly applies the brush to the side
of the bowl. Carefully, very slowly, he traces a short
segment of a curved line. As he studies it critically—

ANOTHER ANGLE—OCCUPATIONAL
THERAPY ROOM

Off to one side, an elderly man, SID GROSS, is carefully hammering a small nail into the corner of a wooden picture frame. He picks it up, examines it, and then hobbles toward Maurie with it.

CLOSE ANGLE—MAURIE

As Sid moves in—

> SID *(exhibiting frame)*
> This what you wanted?

> MAURIE *(examines frame and nods)*
> Not bad. When'll you have it finished?

> SID *(broadly)*
> What's the big rush?

> MAURIE
> I've got to finish it by Christmas.

> SID
> So? This is only September.

> MAURIE
> Stop complaining, or I'll take my business somewhere else.

> SID
> Promises, promises. You make this place a regular sweat-shop.

> MAURIE *(grins)*
> And when you get the frame finished, Sidney . . . get started on that chair.

                    SID (*grumbling*)
We had a good thing going here, 'til you showed
up.

The young woman at the pottery wheel smiles—

                  YOUNG WOMAN
Maybe we should go on strike, Sid.

                      SID
Who can picket?

He leans over and peers at the bowl Maurie is
painting—

                      SID
Rembrandt you ain't.

                    MAURIE
Sorry about that, Mr. Chippendale.

                SID (*shuffling off*)
Work, work . . . all the time, work . . .

        YOUNG WOMAN   (*grins at Maurie*)
He loves it.

          MAURIE (*grinning back*)
When he stops complaining, we're in trouble . . .

Concentrating, he resumes his slow, tedious painting of the bowl.

INT. HOSPITAL MAURIE'S CORRIDOR—
DAY

Jack pushes Maurie's wheel chair out of his room

and down the corridor. Rosie accompanies them, carrying one of the bowls that Maurice has painted. Fully clothed, Maurice appears a little dubious, concerned.

AS THE CAMERA moves back with them—

MAURIE
You sure this is okay with her?

JACK *(impatiently)*
Stop griping, will you! This is what she wanted for her birthday. Though God knows why. And Dr. Walker okayed it. If you didn't want to go, why didn't you say so?

MAURIE
Because I wanted to.

They reach the entry door at the end of the corridor and stop. Rosie places the bowl in Maurie's hands, which lie inertly in his lap. As she makes a last minute adjustment to his tie . . .

ROSIE
Try to behave yourself . . .

As Maurie grins, Jack pushes the wheel chair through the door and along the outer walk-way. Rosie watches as they go off.

EXT TWYMAN HOME—DRIVEWAY—DAY

An ambulance has backed close to the front door of the Twyman home. Two attendants and Jack have just placed the wheel chair, Maurie in it, onto the driveway.

JACK *(to attendants)*
Come back about 11 o'clock . . .

The attendants nod, re-enter the ambulance and drive out of the shot, as Jack pushes the wheel chair toward the front door.

ANGLE AT FRONT DOOR

As Jack and Maurie approach, Carole comes out and moves to them—

CAROLE
Hi, Maurie! . . . you look marvelous!

MAURIE
And I feel better than I look.

JACK
I should hope so. Did you *ever* see a lousy tie like that?

MAURIE
What does *he* know?

CAROLE *(smiling)*
I could answer that in about a minute and a half.

Smiling, Maurie slowly lifts his hands up from his lap, the bowl cradled in them.

CAROLE
For me? . . .

She takes the bowl from Maurie's hands.

MAURIE *(very arty)*

It's an original.

Pleased, Carole studies the bowl and its crude, squiggly design—

CAROLE

It's lovely . . .

(peers closer)

. . . and it's autographed . . . M S . . .

JACK

You're kidding! . . .

He peers closely at the bowl, and then stares at Maurie—

JACK

Who do you think you are? . . . Picasso?

CAROLE *(chiding)*

Oh, Jack . . . stop that . . .

MAURIE *(nodding)*

He's right. I'm not Picasso. Gauguin, maybe. Or that guy with one ear . . .

Carole laughs, as Jack tilts the chair up to get it through the door.

INT. TWYMAN DINING ROOM—NIGHT.

Lisa, now about 7, and Jay, about 5, are just settling into their chairs,—as Jack wheels Maurie up to the

table and sits beside him. Some platters of food are
already on the table. Carole comes in from the
kitchen carrying the final platter, puts it on the
table, sits down, and begins to fill the plates—

MAURIE *(to Jay)*
How do you like school, Jay?

JAY *(grimacing)*
Awful.

LISA *(the authority of age)*
He'll get used to it.

JAY *(firmly)*
Never.

MAURIE *(to Lisa)*
You like school, don't you?

LISA *(as firmly as Jay)*
Nope. But I'm getting used to it.

As Maurie laughs, Carole puts a plate of food before him. As she serves the others, Jack, seated beside Maurie, picks up Maurie's knife and fork and
begins to cut the food into serveable portions.

MAURIE
Hold it . . .

(toward kids)
. . . any basketball fans here?

LISA *(eagerly)*
I am.

JAY

I like football.

JACK

Into each life some rain must fall.

MAURIE *(to Lisa)*

You know what an air ball is?

LISA *(expertly)*

Sure. It's when a shot doesn't hit anything.

MAURIE

And what's a rim shot?

LISA

When it hits the rim and doesn't go in.

MAURIE

Right. And when it comes to feeding me, your father is the air ball and rim shot champion of all time . . .

JACK *(objecting)*

Oh, come now . . .

MAURIE

I've got scars on my lips to prove it. How about you trying it, Lisa?

LISA *(eagerly)*

Sure . . .

She jumps up and runs around the table. Jack gets up and takes his seat at the head of the table, and Lisa sits beside Maurie. She spears a piece of food

with a fork and holds it up in front of Maurie's
mouth. He opens his mouth, and, squinting carefully, Lisa jabs the fork cleanly into his mouth.
Maurie bites it off. As she withdraws the fork—

MAURIE *(chewing)*
That's what I call a clean dunk shot.

Eagerly, Lisa spears another forkful and holds it
up to his mouth—

MAURIE
I've got teeth . . . let me use 'em . . .

He chews a moment, swallows, and then—

MAURIE
Okay . . .

Lisa scores another two points. Chewing, Maurie
glances at Jack—

MAURIE
You taking notes? . . .

EXT. HOSPITAL SUN TERRACE—DAY

This is a broad area, several stories up, jutting out
from the main structure of the hospital. Maurie
is in his wheel chair beside the bordering parapet,
upon which Dorothy sits.

DOROTHY *(conversationally)*
. . . And the apprentice program is working out
very nicely.

MAURIE *(rather tersely)*

Good.

There is a moment's silence. Dorothy is silently aware that he is unresponsive and reflective. After a moment—

MAURIE

What else have you been doing?

DOROTHY

Well, the job takes up most of my time. But I manage to relax once in a while.

MAURIE *(probing)*

Doing what?

DOROTHY *(matter-of-factly)*

Oh, Gladys and I . . . you remember her? . . . we take in a show occasionally. And I manage to visit my folks a couple of times a week . . .

(a little smile)

. . . I don't have too much time on my hands.

MAURIE *(after a beat)*

Don't you have a fellow?

Dorothy manages not to let this disturb her easy, conversational tenor—

DOROTHY

Sure. And I see him every Saturday and Sunday.

MAURIE *(after a beat)*

Dottie . . . I know you don't mean to . . . but you make me a little uncomfortable.

DOROTHY

That's a nice thing to say.

MAURIE

I enjoy your visits. You know that. But with your work, and flying out and back every weekend . . . it doesn't give you much time for anything else.

DOROTHY

What else is there?

MAURIE

It isn't as if we . . . you know what I mean . . .

DOROTHY

Were engaged?

MAURIE

It never got to that, did it?

DOROTHY

Maurie . . . have I ever tried to tell you how to live your life?

MAURIE   *(shakes head)*

That was one of the nice things about you.

DOROTHY

Then, do me a favor, will you? Don't tell me how to live mine.

MAURIE

As long as you live it.

DOROTHY

I do. My own way.

Rosie moves into the shot—

ROSIE

Dr. Walker wants me to get Mo ready for some tests . . .

As Dorothy begins to wheel Maurie toward the door—

MAURIE

I guess they're going to keep testing me until the damn rabbit dies . . .

Dorothy wheels him through the door, Rosie walking alongside.

ANGLE IN CORRIDOR

They move down the corridor and into Maurie's room.

INT. MAURIE'S ROOM

Dorothy stops the wheel chair a few feet from the bed. Rosie removes Maurie's feet from the footrest. Then she puts her hands under Maurie's left arm,—as Dorothy does the same under his right. They lift him to an upright position,—and, as they support him, he manages to take a few awkward steps to the bed. There, he shuffles his feet, turning himself, and sits on the edge of the bed.

ROSIE (matter-of-factly)

Pretty good.

MAURIE (laughing)

Damn good.

Smiling, Dorothy kisses his cheek—

INT. PHYSICAL THERAPY ROOM—DAY

Maurie is on his back on a therapy table, arms extended over his head, his hands holding the handles of a pulley attached to weights. Another pulley, also attached to weights, is fastened to his feet. Alternately, he strains to lift his outstretched arms a few inches. And then his feet, managing to raise his legs a few inches from the table. He stops, as Jack hurriedly enters—

MAURIE
What are you doing up this early?

JACK   *(in haste)*
I have to catch a 9 o'clock plane. I'm flying over to St. Francis for that fund-raising luncheon.

MAURIE
Aren't you playing the Celtics tonight?

JACK   *(nodding)*
I'll be back in time for the game.

MAURIE
You'll be in great shape. Havilcek'll make you look sick.

JACK   *(grinning)*
Won't be the first time. Say hello to Dorothy for me when she gets in this afternoon.

MAURIE   *(nodding)*
How's the Big O these days?

JACK

Great. Always asks about you.

MAURIE *(casually)*

Tell, him, if he's got nothing better to do, why doesn't he drop by this afternoon and we'll rap a little . . .

JACK

Okay . . . he'd like that. I'll call him. See you to-morrow.

As he hurriedly exits—

INT. MAURIE'S ROOM—NIGHT

(By now, Maurie's room has been made very home-like. Some extra cabinets, tables, chairs, etc., many of which were obviously worked on my Maurie. Pictures and other personal belongings embellish the room.) Oscar Robertson and Dorothy are seated beside Maurie's bed in which he is propped up to sitting position.

MAURIE

. . . I hear you've been going great, Big O.

OSCAR *(simply)*

I try, Big Mo.

MAURIE *(to Dorothy)*

Oscar Robertson is the best in the business.

OSCAR *(a little smile)*

That doesn't say much for the business, does it?

DOROTHY

Don't be modest with me. I've seen you play. You're
having a great season.

OSCAR

But those referees are killing us! They've cost us
8 games this season!

DOROTHY

How many games have you lost?

OSCAR

Eight.

Maurie laughs uproariously.

DOROTHY

You're playing the Celtics tonight?

OSCAR *(nods)*

But it's not them I'm worried about. It's the referees . . .

(glances at watch, rises)

. . . I'd better get over to the arena. Can I give
you a lift somewhere, Miss Parsons?

DOROTHY

Thank you, Oscar, but I'll stay awhile.

MAURIE

You'd better take him up on that, Dorothy. I've
got some therapy in a few minutes.

DOROTHY *(rising)*

Okay . . .

(kisses him)

. . . See you tomorrow . . .

OSCAR

Take it easy, Big Mo . . .

MAURIE

You too, Big O . . .

(smiles)

. . . But not on the Celtics . . .

Smiling, Oscar and Dorothy exit.

As Dorothy and Oscar walk toward the entry door—

OSCAR *(perplexed)*

They give him therapy at night?

DOROTHY *(a little smile)*

No. That was just an excuse for you to give me a lift.

OSCAR

I don't get it.

DOROTHY

For months now, almost every time I visit him, he arranges to have one of you fellows here. Wilt, K.C., Willis . . . I've met almost the whole league.

OSCAR

I'm still lost.

DOROTHY *(a bitter-sweet smile)*
He doesn't realize I know what he's doing . . .
He's trying to find a fellow for me . . .

They have reached the entry door and pause.

OSCAR
That's the sort of thing he'd do . . .

They go through entry door to walk-way beyond.
MOVING SHOT—ALONG OUTER WALK-
WAY

OSCAR *(matter-of-factly)*
Where's Jack been all afternoon?

DOROTHY
He flew over to Pennsylvania today. Another fund-
raising luncheon . . .

(smiles)
. . . But he'll be back in time for the game.

OSCAR
I don't know how he does it.

They continue walking silently and go through
the main hospital corridor area.

INT. HOSPITAL MAIN CORRIDOR AREA—
MOVING SHOT

They walk silently for a moment and then she
looks up—

DOROTHY *(quietly)*
Why *does* he do it?

OSCAR

I don't know.

DOROTHY *(reflectively)*
All these years. He's never wavered. As if what he's
done for Maurie was the most natural thing in the
world. To take that on, along with his family and
his own career. I've often wondered. Why?

OSCAR *(quietly)*
I don't know.

DOROTHY
But you've known Maurie and Jack for a long time.
You must have wondered, too . . .

OSCAR *(straightforwardly)*
I've never wondered about it at all.

Dorothy looks at him, openly skeptical. They
have reached the main hospital entrance and go
through the door.

EXT. HOSPITAL ENTRANCE

Oscar's car is in the driveway, right outside the entrance. They cross the sidewalk and move to the
car. Oscar opens the door and assists Dorothy in.
He goes around to the driver's side and enters.

INT. OSCAR'S CAR

DOROTHY *(still skeptical, looks at him)*
You're not being honest, Oscar. You're a sensitive
man. You must have thought about it.

Oscar sits for a moment deeply preoccupied and then—

OSCAR *(soberly)*
No. I never did. Because if I ever wondered why Jack did it . . . I'd have to wonder why I didn't . . .

As Dorothy stares at him deeply moved, he starts the engine—

LARGER ANGLE

The car drives off.

INT. TWYMAN DEN—DAY

Jack is on the phone, seated at his desk—bills and papers spread out in front of him.

JACK
. . . Okay, Tom . . . try to get somebody over there this afternoon to measure him . . . oh, a few pairs of slacks and some sport shirts . . . and nothing tacky . . . he doesn't want to look like a gypsy when he has visitors . . . right, rush the clothes . . .

(grins)
. . . and take your time with the bill . . . thanks, Tom . . .

He hangs up and is doing some work on his accounts as Carole enters—

JACK *(looking up)*

Honey . . . if that check comes in while I'm away, from the stock I sold, please deposit it to Maurie's account right away. I've got a lot of checks out.

CAROLE

Okay. When are you leaving?

JACK

We've got a charter flight at 4 o'clock.

CAROLE

With the airlines on strike, Dorothy won't get to see Maurie this week.

JACK

I guess not. But she'll probably call him . . .

INT. OCCUPATIONAL THERAPY ROOM— DAY

In his wheel chair, sandpaper taped to his hands, Maurie is sanding a large picture frame. Dorothy is seated next to him. Nearby, Sid is putting together a small table.

MAURIE

. . . And then I'm going to lacquer over a whole bunch of pictures of Jack, and give this to Jack's boy for Christmas.

DOROTHY

Jay'll love that.

MAURIE *(grinning)*

He'd like it better if Jack were scoring touchdowns . . .

(glances at Sid)

. . . You think that table is going to be high enough?

Sid looks up, as Dorothy studies the table—

DOROTHY
It looks about right to me.

MAURIE
Not to me. That was supposed to be 24 inches high, Sid.

SID
So?

MAURIE
So that doesn't look like 24 inches.

SID
So it will when I put the casters on.

MAURIE *(grinning)*
So I'll keep my big mouth shut.

SID
Promises, promises.

DOROTHY *(laughing)*
Sidney, you're doing just fine.

SID
I know that. Tell him.

DOROTHY
And every time I watch my television set, sitting on your table, I'll think of you.

MAURIE

And when the table collapses and wrecks your set,
think of him.

DOROTHY

Maurie . . . I'm sorry . . . but I think I'd better
get started. It's a long drive back to New York.

MAURIE *(agreeably)*

Sure, sweetie, I know.

DOROTHY *(to Sid)*

See you next week, Sidney.

SID

That'll be nice.

DOROTHY *(to Maurie)*

Do you want to go back to your room?

MAURIE

No, I'll work a while.

Dorothy kisses him—

DOROTHY

See you soon, honey . . .

And she exits. Maurie sits for a moment, thinking.

SID

Now, *that's* a girl!

MAURIE

Yeah.

SID

The airlines don't fly. She drives all that way.
That's what I call nice!

MAURIE

Nice? Miraculous. She doesn't drive.

As Sid looks at him, quizzically—

MAURIE

Sid, wheel me out to the terrace.

SID *(aghast)*

You outa your mind? It's freezing out there!

MAURIE

Wheel me, Sid . . .

SID

Maybe *you're* an Eskimo! Not *me!*

MAURIE *(firmly)*

Sidney . . .

Sidney shrugs, gets up, and, in his customary shuf-
fle, begins to wheel Maurie toward the door. He
stops near the door, opens a cupboard, takes out a
blanket and carefully tucks it around Maurie.
Then he throws a blanket around his own shoulders and wheels Maurie out.

ANGLE ON TERRACE

It is a gray, bleak day and some leaves and papers
scuttle across the terrace in the cold wind. Sid
wheels Maurie through the door and stops—

                    SID *(cringing)*
Okay, now can we go back in?

                    MAURIE
Over to the edge . . .

                    SID
Good news at last! You're going to jump!

Grumbling, he wheels Maurie to the parapet. Sid
shrivels up under his blanket.

                    SID *(sourly)*
Miami Beach this isn't . . .

Impassive, Maurie sits there looking off and down.

                    SID
You're a nut!

Maurie does not react. He just looks down—

ANGLE OVER MAURIE AND SID—TO-
WARD HOSPITAL DRIVEWAY

In the distance, below, we see a car parked at the
curb of the driveway. Dorothy exits from the hospital door and, as she moves toward the car, a man
gets out, comes around to the side of the car and
waits for her. He is a nice looking, well-dressed
man. Dorothy reaches the car and, for a moment,
they talk. Then, the man puts his arm around
Dorothy's shoulder, gives her a reassuring squeeze,
opens the car door and she gets in. He moves to
the other side, gets in, and the car drives off.

CLOSE SHOT—MAURIE

As he watches, a little smile plays across his face,
—and he takes a deep, contented breath. Then he
looks up at Sidney who, huddled under his blanket, has been oblivious to the scene below—

MAURIE *(very relaxed)*
Okay, Sid, let's go in now.

SID *(grousing)*
Just what did we accomplish by all this?

LARGER ANGLE

As Sid turns the chair and starts back toward the
hospital—

MAURIE
A little fresh air is good for you, Sid . . .

SID *(broadly sardonic)*
Oho! Now he's making prescriptions, like a
doctor! . . .

And he wheels Maurie back into the hospital.

INT. MAURIE'S ROOM—NIGHT

Maurie is in an oxygen tent. Concerned and
serious, Rosie is fiddling with some piece of equipment beside the bed. Mr. and Mrs. Stokes stand
beside the bed looking at Maurie, deeply troubled.
Finally, they turn and exit the room.

ANGLE—CORRIDOR—MOVING SHOT

CAMERA MOVES BACK down corridor with Mr. and Mrs. Stokes to near the nurses' station where Jack is standing with Dr. Walker.

ANGLE ON JACK AND DR. WALKER

As Mr. and Mrs. Stokes join them—

DR. WALKER

I'd like to call in Dr. Killian, from St. Elizabeth's, for consultation.

JACK

Is it that serious?

DR. WALKER

Today, pneumonia usually isn't. Under normal circumstances, we can handle it. But it's been three days now . . .

MRS. STOKES

You *can* do something, can't you?

DR. WALKER

I think so, but we have to handle it differently than with an ordinary patient. Maurie has been under a great physical strain all these years. In his condition, an illness that an ordinary patient would throw off easily could have some residual effect. We have to be careful not to overburden his heart. I'll get Killian and his team over here right way.

As he moves away, the Stokes and Jack reflect their concern—

INT.—MAURIE'S ROOM—DAY

Maurie is in bed,—the typewriter on the bed-table across his torso, his fingers suspended over the keyboard by the pulley sling. A sheet of paper is in the typewriter carriage. The door opens and Jack enters. He looks and moves like a tired man.

JACK   *(a bit flatly)*

How's it going, Mo? . . .

MAURIE

Okay. But you look whipped.

Jack sinks into a chair, wearily.

JACK

Earl the Pearl ran my tail off last night.

MAURIE   *(a little smile)*

You ought to get more sleep.

JACK   *(yawning)*

I get enough.

MAURIE

You didn't last week, when I was sick.

JACK

How would you know?

MAURIE

I wasn't that far gone. You were around. I heard you. What were you worried about?

JACK   *(sardonically)*

I wasn't worried. I just wanted to make sure they

weren't wasting any of our money.

He yawns again and rests his head against the back of the chair. After a moment—

MAURIE

How *are* we fixed for money?

JACK

Okay.

MAURIE

How much have we got?

JACK

You've never asked me that before.

MAURIE

I'd like to know.

JACK

Why?

MAURIE

Curious.

JACK

Oh, thirty, forty thousand.

MAURIE *(staring at him)*

You're kidding?

JACK

Don't get excited. That doesn't last long.

For a long moment, Maurie digests this soberly.

MAURIE

Jack . . . where would that money go if something happened to me?

JACK *(sleepily)*

Nothing's going to happen to you.

MAURIE

But if it did.

JACK

What are you expecting to happen?

MAURIE *(a little smile)*

Who knows? I could get hit by a truck.

JACK *(yawning again)*

Well, the first time I see a truck out in the hall, we'll talk about it. Okay?

MAURIE *(after a beat)*

Jack . . . can I make a Will?

JACK

I don't think so.

MAURIE

Why? Because you're my guardian?

JACK

Hell, that's got nothing to do with it. To make a Will, you have to be of sound mind. And you're nuts!

Maurie grins and stares at the typewriter—

MAURIE

Do I have to have a lawyer, or can I write one out myself?

There is no answer from Jack, and Maurie glances toward him. Jack is sound asleep. And, as Maurie looks at Jack, an affectionate smile crosses his face. Then he turns back to the typewriter and frowns in concentration, as his fingers, slowly and with effort, begin to peck at the keys.

INT.—RECEPTION AREA AND DESK—
MAURIE'S FLOOR—DAY

Jack and Rosie stand near the floor desk—

JACK

. . . But why isn't he in physical therapy?

ROSIE

Dr. Walker has eased him off a little since the pneumonia. I guess he's a little slower coming back from it than most people would be. But he keeps busy, doing *something* . . .

INT. CHILDREN'S THERAPY ROOM—DAY

Maurie is in his wheel chair, near the end of the room. A boy, about 10, in hospital robe, stands near Maurie, dribbling a basketball. Another boy, about the same age, stands nearby, within a wheeled stroller, which he leans on with both hands. Three or four other kids are also watching, attentively. A crude hoop has been attached to the wall, about six feet up. Maurie watches the boy practice his dribble.

MAURIE

. . . No, Pete . . . you've got your fingers all pressed together. Spread them out . . . like this . . .

Maurie lifts his hand a few inches and slowly spreads his fingers. The boy watches, spreads his fingers, and bounces the ball a few times.

MAURIE

That's better . . .

Jack enters the room and strolls toward them—

JACK

I didn't know the Knicks were in town.

PETE

We're the third floor Tigers . . .

MAURIE

And we're getting ready for the big game against the fourth floor Sharks. Let's try that pass to Johnny . . .

Pete dribbles a couple of times and then, with both hands, passes the ball to Johnny, who is inside the stroller. Johnny releases one hand from the stroller bar and catches the ball against his chest. Then he bounces the ball once with his free hand, takes a tentative step while leaning against the stroller with his other hand and, one-handed, throws the ball to the hoop. It goes in cleanly.

JACK

Wow!

MAURIE *(a broad grin)*
He's got an eye like an eagle! Never misses!

As Johnny's ball goes through the hoop, the smallest kid in the room, who barely comes up to Jack's waist, retrieves the ball, which is almost as big as he is. He has to hold it cradled in both of his arms. He comes with it to Jack and looks up at Jack.

LITTLE KID
Could you show me how to do a dunk shot?

JACK *(grinning)*
Sure . . .

He reaches down, grasps the tyke by the waist, and lifts him, as if he were weightless, to where the kid's body is above the rim of the hoop. The kid is suspended above it still holding the ball in both arms.

JACK
Dunk . . .

The kid drops the ball through the hoop. As Jack lowers the kid back to the floor—

JACK
You dunk great, pal . . .

Pete retrieves the ball and throws it to Jack.

PETE

Show us how the pros do it . . .

Jack dribbles the ball twice and flips it to the hoop. It hits the rim and bounces off.

MAURIE

Let's get out of here. You're undoing all of my good work . . .

(to the kids)

. . . We'll do some more tomorrow . . .

As the kids pass the ball around, Jack wheels Maurie out—

ANGLE IN CORRIDOR—MOVING SHOT

MAURIE

It was nice of you to miss that shot . . .

JACK (grinning)

What makes you so sure it was deliberate?

INT. MAURIE'S ROOM—DAY

As Jack wheels Maurie in—

MAURIE

. . . You don't miss many.

JACK

I'm not going to miss any.

As Maurie stares at him, quizzically, Jack plops into a chair—

JACK

I'm retiring.

MAURIE   *(surprised, skeptical)*

Come on . . .

JACK   *(nodding)*

I'm hanging them up last game of the season.

MAURIE

Why? You're averaging over 20 points a game.

JACK

That's the right time to go. I've had 11 pretty good years.

MAURIE

Great years.

JACK   *(a little grin)*

I didn't think you'd noticed.

MAURIE

What are you going to do?

JACK

Haven't thought about that yet.

MAURIE

Most of the guys are working on something, while they're playing. Moonlighting off-season. Making plans. But you've spent so much time butting into my business . . . you haven't prepared anything for your retirement, have you?

JACK   *(ignoring the question)*

Mo . . . they're giving me a night that last
game . . .

MAURIE

That's the least they can do . . .

(sincerely)

. . . It'll be a great night for you, Jack.

JACK

For us.

MAURIE

What do I have to do with it?

JACK

I want you to come.

MAURIE

To the arena? . . .

(shakes head)

. . . Forget it.

JACK

Dr. Walker says it's okay. And I want you there.

MAURIE   *(firmly)*

No chance.

JACK   *(just as firmly)*

Mo . . .

MAURIE   *(interrupting, earnestly)*

Look, Jack . . . don't ask me. I'm not going to be

wheeled into that arena . . . in front of all those
people.

> JACK   (controlled irritation)
>
> . . . You make a deal with me, and then back
> out?

> MAURIE   (honestly perplexed)
>
> What deal?

> JACK   (scathing)
>
> You once said . . .

> (mimicking)
>
> . . . 'How will I ever be able to thank you' . . .
> I said I'd tell you . . . I've told you . . . and
> you back out.

Maurie stares soberly at Jack for just a moment.
And then a little smile touches him—

> MAURIE
>
> When's the game?

FULL SHOT—INT. ROYALS' ARENA—NIGHT

The place is jammed. The Royals and the Warriors are just finishing their warm-ups and strag-
gling back to their respective benches.

CLOSER ANGLE—ROYALS' BENCH

As the players take their seats. In the first row,
immediately behind the bench, and slightly raised,

we see Dorothy, Carole, Lisa, Jay and Mr. and Mrs. Stokes.

ANOTHER ANGLE ON THE FLOOR—RAKING THE BENCHES

Between the team benches, the public address announcer sits before a microphone—

ANNOUNCER

Ladies and Gentlemen . . . tonight's lineup for the Warriors! . . .

INT. MEDIUM SHOT—REAR DOOR—CORRIDOR BEHIND GRANDSTAND

Rosie wheels Maurie down the corridor and stops near passageway to the arena. This is not a public area, and there are only a few behind-the-scenes staff moving about in the background.

CLOSE SHOT—MAURIE & ROSIE

Off-stage, we hear the announcer presenting, in quick succession, the Warrior players. As the announcements continue, Maurie sits there, tensely. It is a deeply moving moment for him,— his first return to the arena where he performed so spectacularly. He is fully dressed in a new suit, his hands gripping, as much as they can, the arms of his wheel chair. If Rosie feels or senses the emotions that must be clutching Maurie, she does not show it as she calmly stands there. Maurie listens as the announcer begins to introduce members of

the Royals. Maurie is almost apprehensive as he
glances up at Rosie—

MAURIE

Do I look all right?

ROSIE *(typically)*

The suit fits great. For you to look any better,
we'd have to do plastic surgery.

But Maurie does not typically respond to Rosie's
joshing.

MAURIE

Wheel me in while he's introducing the players
. . . and no one'll notice me.

ROSIE

Don't be a back-seat driver . . .

And she just stands there, behind Maurie's wheel-
chair, waiting.

ANGLE ON FLOOR

The Warriors are back at their bench. Three
Royals, already announced, are at center court, as—

ANNOUNCER

. . . the Big O, Oscar Robertson! . . .

There is an enthusiastic reaction from the crowd
as Robertson jogs from the bench and takes his
position alongside the team.

ANNOUNCER

. . . And now, with a deep regret that I am sure

all of you, all of the players, and fans everywhere
share with me, may I introduce for the last time
. . . at forward . . . Jack Twyman! . . .

There is an enormous reaction from the crowd.
The applause crescendos as Jack jogs out to join
the team. The players of both teams join in the
tribute to him. It lasts for several moments and,
gradually, dies down.

ANNOUNCER

. . . We are fortunate tonight. Our sadness at saying good-bye to Jack is greatly relieved by our
happiness at being able to say 'hello' once again,
to . . . Big Mo! . . . Maurie Stokes! . . .

MEDIUM ANGLE—TOWARD PASSAGE-
WAY

There is a strange quietness over the arena. And
then, suddenly, Rosie pushes Maurie's wheel
chair out of the shadows of the passageway into
the full lights of the arena floor. There is still a
momentary hush. But, as Rosie wheels him on to
the floor toward the teams, an avalanche of sound
wells up from the crowd.

ANOTHER ANGLE—CENTER OF FLOOR

As the crowd rises to its feet, the place reverber-
ates with sound. Rosie wheels Maurie to the lineup of Royals and stops Maurie's wheel chair
beside Jack,—who grins down at him.

CLOSE ANGLE—MAURIE

He is almost trembling as the emotions of the crowd envelop him. Barely able to control herself, Rosie pats his shoulder and walks off. Maurie is seemingly perplexed by her abrupt abandonment.

LARGER ANGLE—ON FLOOR

As the ovation continues, the players of both teams move to their respective benches. Jack gets behind Maurie's wheel chair and, as the applause continues, wheels Maurie to the end of the Royals' bench and puts his chair in position beside it, as the crowd cheers.

CLOSE ANGLE—MAURIE & JACK

Maurie glances up at Jack—

MAURIE

Give me a hand . . .

Jack braces himself in front of Maurie, places his hands under Maurie's armpits and draws him to an erect position. And then, Maurie slowly shuffles his feet until he has managed to turn himself and is facing the crowd. He stands erect for a moment and then manages a shallow but obvious bow. The ovation crescendos, as Maurie again shuffles his feet, slowly turning,—and Jack assists him back into his chair. The ovation continues as Dorothy sits beside Maurie and takes his hand in hers. . . .

INT. MAURIE'S ROOM—NIGHT

Jack wheels Maurie in and then takes a deep breath—

JACK *(tentatively)*

Well . . . that's that.

Maurie looks up at Jack for a moment, soberly thoughtful—

MAURIE

Jack . . . tell me something. And don't bull me. What *are* you going to do now?

JACK

I'm going to get some sleep. I'm bushed.

MAURIE *(seriously)*

Cut it out, Jack. Have you got anything lined up?

JACK

You been worrying about that?

MAURIE *(quietly candid)*

Yes.

JACK

Well . . . the people at ABC have been talking to me . . . about taking a shot at the play-off games next week.

MAURIE

Doing what?

JACK *(a little archly)*

What they call expert commentary.

MAURIE

They're going to put *you* on the air? It won't be fit to breathe.

JACK *(a little grin)*

That may be. But I'm going to do a couple of the games . . . the Lakers and the Celtics . . . with Chris Schenkel.

MAURIE *(interested, pleased)*

On the level? That's terrific. You'd better get some sleep, so you won't look like 20 miles of detour.

JACK *(a little smile, nods)*

Yeah . . .

He moves slowly toward the door, pauses, and looks back soberly—

JACK *(quietly)*

Mo . . . thanks for helping make my night great.

MAURIE *(simply)*

Thanks for making my last 10 years great.

For the first time, the two men are leveling with each other. Jack glances around the room for a moment, and then he looks at Maurie—

JACK *(softly)*

Good night, Mo . . .

MAURIE

Good night, Jack . . .

Jack exits,—and we hold briefly on Maurie, relaxed, contented.

INT. LOS ANGELES FORUM

The Lakers and the Celtics are warming up.

CLOSE ANGLE—JACK AND CHRIS SCHEN-KEL—BROADCAST BOOTH

They are seated before microphones—

SCHENKEL

. . . And to set the background of this important
game for you, we're very happy to have with us
one of the all-time greats of the NBA . . . Jack
Twyman . . .

JACK

. . . Thank you, Chris. It's an important game
alright. And it should be a great one. We'll see
some interesting matchups tonight . . . Jerry
West against KC Jones . . . Baylor against Hav-
licek . . . Sam Jones against Walt Hazzard . . .
and, of course, Bill Russell under the basket
against everybody . . .

SCHENKEL

What do you especially look for tonight?

JACK

Well, the Celtics have great speed. I don't think
the Lakers can run with them. But in Baylor and
West they have two great shooters who are hard
to stop . . .

INT. MAURIE'S ROOM

In his wheel chair, thoroughly engrossed, Maurie intently watches the television screen,—Rosie perched on the edge of the bed beside him. She is enthralled—

ROSIE *(excitedly)*
Look at Jack! Isn't he *handsome?*

MAURIE
You watching the same television I am?

ROSIE *(ignoring him)*
And he *sounds* so good!

MAURIE
I can't understand a word he's saying.

ROSIE *(chastising)*
Now you just stop that, Mo!

MAURIE *(also chastising)*
What did you think he'd be? Lousy? . . .

He never takes his eyes off the screen. Despite his teasing with Rosie, he is obviously attentively studying and listening to Jack.

INT. LOS ANGELES FORUM

Game action.

CLOSE ANGLE—JACK

JACK
. . . Unless Ellis can draw Russell away from the

basket, the Lakers will have to start hitting on those outside shots . . .

INT. LOS ANGELES FORUM

Game action.

INT. MAURIE'S ROOM

As Jack's staccato commentary plays over the scene—

ROSIE

The way Jack explains it, even I can understand it! . . .

Maurie's eyes are still glued to the set. And it is obvious that he likes what he is seeing and hearing.

INT. LOS ANGELES FORUM

An exciting scoring play,—followed shortly by the final buzzer.

CLOSE SHOT—JACK AND SCHENKEL

SCHENKEL

. . . Well, Jack . . . your hunch was right. To-night, at least, Boston's fast break was too much for the Lakers. Do you think the Celtics can do it again Friday night?

JACK

I think we'll see a different game then, Chris. I look for LaRusso to crash the boards more. And with his strength he may be able to offset some of

Russell's great defensive work. And I think we'll
see the Lakers flood one side of the court on offense so West can work one-on-one against KC
Jones. KC is a truly great player. But Jerry has a
considerable height advantage and, one-on-one, he
should score points . . .

INT. MAURIE'S ROOM

Although still watching and listening, Maurie is
more relaxed in his chair. And he reflects a deep
contentment at what he has seen and heard.

ROSIE

You know something, Mo? I never thought I'd
get this interested. I can hardly wait for that game
Friday. He really did do good, didn't he?

MAURIE *(quietly)*

He was great. No one could do it better . . .

CLOSE SHOT—JACK AND SCHENKEL

SCHENKEL

. . . And so, that about does it for tonight. Hope
you'll be with us Friday night for the second
game . . .

(to Jack)

. . . It's great having you with us, Jack. And I
look forward to working with you again Friday . . .

JACK

Thanks, Chris . . . I'm looking forward to it,
too . . .

(hesitates)
. . . Would the FCC put me in jail if I throw a little personal note in? . . .

SCHENKEL *(smiles)*
I think I know what you're getting at. Go ahead, Jack . . .

Jack looks into the camera, with a little grin—

JACK
Good night, pal . . .

CLOSE SHOT—ROSIE

A big, pleased smile seizes her face—

ROSIE
Oh, wasn't that *nice* of Jack! . . .

She glances happily over toward Maurie,—and the CAMERA PANS TO HIM.

His head is slumped on his chest.

LARGER ANGLE

Quickly, all business, Rosie jumps from the side of the bed, grabs a stethoscope hanging above it, attaches it to her ears and applies it to Maurie's chest,—several times, in several places. And then, very slowly, she straightens up, utterly desolated. She looks at him for a long moment and then bends down and kisses his cheek. Then she leaves the room.

FULL BOOM SHOT—INT. LOS ANGELES
FORUM—ARENA FLOOR—NIGHT

Except for a house light, dimly illuminating the
floor, the rest of the vast arena is in shadow. The
CAMERA MOVES SLOWLY across the floor and
up to the third or fourth row. Alone, Jack sits
there, arms resting on his knees—drained and immersed in his thoughts.

ANOTHER ANGLE—FROM BEHIND JACK
—TOWARD ARENA FLOOR

As Jack sits there, a figure appears out of the shadows on the other side of the floor and comes slowly
across the floor toward Jack—Oscar Robertson. He
moves the few steps up the aisle and sits beside
Jack.

CLOSE TWO SHOT—JACK & ROBERTSON
For a long moment, the two men just sit there.

OSCAR   (softly)
When you weren't at the hotel, I thought you
might be here . . .

Jack doesn't react or turn. In a whisper, to himself,
as if Oscar weren't there—

JACK
He made a Will . . . ⅓ to his folks . . . ⅓ to the
nurses and therapists . . . and ⅓ to St. Francis for
scholarships . . .

OSCAR *(after a beat, nods)*
Sounds like him.

Another long moment—

OSCAR
You a drinking man?

(a bare shake of Jack's head)
. . . me neither . . .

(a beat)
. . . but you know what we're going to do? We're gonna have a drink to Mo . . .

Jack finally turns his head and looks at Oscar—

OSCAR *(softly)*
Isn't that what you do? You toast a winner . . .

JACK *(very softly)*
He was, wasn't he? . . .

LARGER ANGLE—BOOM SHOT

Oscar rises, and then Jack. They move slowly down to the floor and begin to cross it, toward the passageway at the end. The two men walk slowly, side by side, in the dim, shadowy light. As they approach the passageway at the end of the floor, near the basket, Oscar puts his arm around Jack's shoulder,—and they disappear through the passageway.

FADE OUT